Pat Collins CM

UNVEILING THE HEART

HOW TO OVERCOME EVIL
IN THE CHRISTIAN LIFE

VERITAS

First published 1995 by
Veritas Publications
7-8 Lower Abbey Street
Dublin 1

ISBN 1 85390 239 X

British Library Cataloguing
in Publication Data.
A catalogue record for
this book is available
from the British Library.

The cover illustration is based on an image of the Devil from the Book of Kells.

Cover design by Bill Bolger
Printed in the Republic of Ireland by Betaprint Ltd, Dublin

CONTENTS

Dedicated to John, Peter and Marie

INTRODUCTION

In the twentieth century, instead of dying of natural causes, hundreds of millions of our fellow human beings have died as a result of human aggression. Besides the terrible killings, countless millions of other people have become the victims of exploitation, crime and injustice. There are many ways of explaining such evils – historical, psychological, political, economical, philosophical etc. For example, in his book *The Ghost in the Machine*,[1] the late Arthur Koestler tried to understand evil in purely biological terms. He believed that human beings had evolved so fast that there was a split in their brains between the older, more animal-like limbic cortex, and the newer, more intellectual neo-cortex. He asserted that this 'schizo-physiology', to use his awkward term, was the origin of the paranoid streak which accounts for the blood-drenched pages of human history. Explanations like this may explain the mystery of evil to a certain extent, but ultimately they fail to get to the heart of the matter. Christians believe that evil cannot be properly understood without taking into account what the Church has to say about the existence and activity of the Devil.

Having asserted the existence of the Evil One, Pope Paul VI once said, 'The question of the Devil and the influence he can exert on individual persons as well as on communities, whole societies or events, is a very important chapter of Catholic doctrine. It is given little attention today, though it should be studied again.' Having made that comment, he went on to add, 'our doctrine,' however, 'becomes uncertain, obscured as it is by the darkness surrounding the Devil.'[2] This book is intended to be a modest raid on the inarticulate. As I was writing it, I had the disconcerting sense that my religious imagination exceeded both my ability as a writer and my obedience as a Christian. But I was encouraged to continue by a paradoxical saying attributed to G. K. Chesterton: 'If a thing is worth doing, it is worth doing badly!'

So, while the book is neither comprehensive nor profound, it aims to provide some pointers as to how Christians can overcome evil of different kinds. The opening chapters look at the notion of diabolical evil from a number of perspectives – experiential, scientific, psychological and doctrinal. The final chapters propose various ways of countering the tactics of the Evil One, by means of ongoing transformation in Christ. They include practical suggestions about overcoming the evils of sin, temptation and addiction, by means of such things as inner healing, discernment of spirits, asceticism and prayer.

I want to thank a number of people. Firstly, I owe a debt of gratitude to Kristina Cooper and Rochelle Gibler, who are the editors of English magazines entitled *Goodnews* and *Miracles* respectively. In the summer of 1993 they urged me to write about the ways in which Christians can recognise and overcome evil in their lives. I'm also grateful to Fr Chris O'Donnell OCarm, who read the draft of what was at first intended to be a five-chapter booklet on the nature of diabolical evil. He not only made many helpful comments, but also suggested that there was a need for extra material. As a result, nine extra chapters have been added. Next, I want to say a sincere 'thank you' to Marie, Angela and Mena who gave me encouragement, listened when I was thinking out loud, and made helpful suggestions during the writing of the book. Lastly, I want to express my gratitude to Veritas for their kindness to me over the years, and to Fiona Biggs, in particular, for her understanding and co-operation.

1

A TIME OF ADVERSITY

Some years ago, while travelling by train to a prayer meeting in Weston School of Theology in Cambridge, Massachusetts, I had, what for me was a unique experience. Inwardly I seemed to hear a prophecy which was addressed to me personally. Although I didn't understand it at the time, I was able to remember it afterwards.

> Leave the city with its proud flags and go to the breach in the wall.
> Go and stand in the breach, the place of insecurity.
> Stand in the breach where the wind blows,
> where the jackal cries
> and where the enemy enters under the cloak of darkness.
> Stand in the breach and intercede for yourself and for my people.
> Stand in the breach and listen to my word.
> Then call my people to the breach to rebuild the walls of Jerusalem.

Because I was anxious to discern whether these words were inspired by the Spirit or not, I decided to do something that I have advised others not to do; I cut the scriptures. I made up my mind that if my finger was on the words, 'Rebuild the walls of Jerusalem,' I would take it that the word of prophecy had come from the Lord rather than from myself or the Evil One. After a brief prayer for help, I opened my bible at random. My finger was on Psalm 51:58, which reads, 'Rebuild the walls of Jerusalem!' Since that memorable day I have often pondered in a prayerful way what the implications of the Lord's word might be. Briefly put, these are some of my tentative conclusions.

At the present time, the Church is undergoing a time of painful adversity and affliction. The walls of its spiritual life have been badly breached. As a result, the Catholic community has become particularly susceptible to the attacks of the Evil One. It seems to me that the Lord is calling us, in an urgent and prophetic way, to do three interrelated things. Firstly, to recognise the true nature of this diabolical danger. Secondly, to stand in the places of greatest vulnerability in order to defend the Church from attack. Thirdly, to work for the renewal of the Church by identifying and repairing the breaches, in our own personal lives especially, and in the wider community as well.

Recognising and naming the danger

In recent years I have had a growing conviction that the current affliction of the Church is diabolical in origin. To those who deny the Devil's existence, this might seem to be a fundamentalist and sensationalist point of view. But, as I will try to show in the opening chapters of this book, there are good reasons for adopting this point of view.

Following Vatican II we had wonderful blueprints for change and renewal. But, as the psalmist has warned us, 'Unless the Lord build the house, in vain do the labourers build' (Ps 127:1). Unfortunately, we were a bit like St Peter, who promised Jesus so much. Despite our good intentions and hard work, we often failed to implement the vision of the council fathers. During the intervening years the Lord has allowed us to be afflicted in many ways. It was as if he were saying to us as he once said to Peter, 'Listen! Satan has demanded to sift you all like wheat, but I have prayed for you that your own faith may not fail; and you, when you have turned back, strengthen your brothers' (Lk 22:31).

During an apparition in 1982 in Medjugorje, Our Lady referred to the diabolical nature of this affliction. 'Excuse me for saying this,' she is reported to have said, 'but you must realise that Satan exists. One day he appeared before the throne of God and asked permission to submit the Church to a period of trial. God gave him permission to submit the Church to a period of trial. God gave him permission to try the Church for one century. This century is under the power of the Devil....but even now he is beginning to lose his power and has become aggressive. He is destroying marriages, creating divisions among priests and is responsible for obsessions and murder. You must protect yourselves against these things through fasting and prayer, especially community prayer.'[1]

Surely the Evil One has mounted a massive attack on the Church in recent years. He has successfully exploited our personal and collective weaknesses by means of illusions, false inspirations and subtle temptations to sin. As a result, the walls of the Church's spiritual life have been breached. The Trojan horse of secularism and worldliness has entered the life of the community. It is evident in the à la carte approach to morality and belief. As a missioner and confessor I have become aware of widespread moral relativism, e.g. in the whole area of sexual values and conduct. I suspect that recent scandals, which have been widely reported in the media, may only be the tip of a larger iceberg. I'm also aware that in financial and business dealings there is widespread dishonesty. As a college lecturer I have become conscious of a tendency to water down the teachings of the Church in order to adapt them to contemporary ways of thinking. For example, many people reject the Church's belief in hell or in the Devil's existence. They mistakenly maintain that the latter is nothing but a psychological projection of human evil.

Pope Paul VI seemed to acknowledge this state of affairs. Not only did he assert the reality of the Devil's existence, he stated that 'It was believed that after the second Vatican Council there would be a day of sunshine in the history of the Church. There came instead a day of clouds, storm and darkness, of search and uncertainty. This came through an adverse power, his name is the Devil.' Is it any surprise therefore that, no matter what statistical data one chooses to look at, the Church in western countries seems to be in a state of crisis?[2] For example, there has been a significant fall in vocations to the priesthood and religious life, and although the Lord commissioned the Church to 'go into the whole world to proclaim the good news to the whole of creation' (Mk 16:15), instead of gaining new members it is losing many of the members it already has, especially in deprived urban areas. For example, in some of the less well-off suburbs of Dublin, practice rates are as low as ten per cent. This is a sad and ironic fact when one considers that Jesus came, as he said himself, 'to bring good news to the poor' (Lk 4:18).

9

Defending ourselves and the Church

Having recognised the diabolical nature of the attack on ourselves and the Church, we need to engage in so-called 'spiritual warfare' in order to defend ourselves. The New Testament talks about this form of combat on a number of occasions. In 1 Timothy 1:18 we read, 'fight the good fight.' Ephesians 6:11 says, 'Put on the whole armour of God, so that you may be able to stand against the wiles of the Devil.' In 2 Corinthians 10:3-4, St Paul confidently asserts that 'We do not wage war according to human standards; for the weapons of our warfare are not merely human, but they have power to destroy strongholds [of evil].' There are many inspiring images of this kind of defensive warfare in both biblical and Church history.

For example, I find one such incident particularly uplifting. In 1565 the Sultan of Turkey commanded 200 ships and 40,000 men to attack the island of Malta, the gateway to Christian Europe. It was defended by 600 Knights of St John and around 8,000 men. The ferocious attacks began on 18 May. By the end of June it was clear that the fort of St Elmo, one of two large fortifications on the island, couldn't hold out much longer. When he heard that it was in imminent danger of falling, the Christian leader, Jean Parisot de la Valette, asked for volunteers, men who would go and defend the stronghold. Fifteen knights, many soldiers and some local Maltese men came forward. 'They received the Holy Sacrament, they embraced one another, and they encouraged each other with such words of consolation as only brave men about to die can use.' After making heroic efforts to defend the fort, every one of these valiant men was killed and the enemy finally took possession of St Elmo on 23 June.

Some time later the Turks turned their attention to the principal Christian fortress of St Angelo. Having sustained withering cannon fire, the walls were breached in many places. Ernle Bradford has described what happened in his fascinating book, *The Great Siege: Malta 1565.*[3] The Turks attacked again and again, but without success. The knights and their companions defended the fortress, and especially the breaches in the walls, with extraordinary bravery. Even the wounded La Valette took part. On one occasion the Grand Master said, 'I am seventy-one. And how is it possible for a man of my age to die more gloriously than in the midst of my friends and brothers, in the service of God?' And over the next two months he often urged on his troops saying, 'No man can end his life more gloriously than in defence of the Faith.' Finally, on 8 September, the feast of the Nativity of the Virgin, the siege was raised. And so ended one of the most heroic episodes in European military history. Christendom had been saved. However, La Valette was not slow to remind the small number of survivors that they owed their deliverance to God, and not to human intervention.

During the present time of affliction, we should defend the Church from the attacks of the Evil One, with something like the same conviction, dedication and selflessness as those courageous knights of old. Later in the book we will look at some of the ways in which this can be done. At the moment, however, I'd like to advert to the importance of intercessory prayer in spiritual combat. When he was in Ireland in 1979, Pope John Paul II spoke in a prophetic way about the ongoing need for prayer. 'Your country,' he observed at Limerick, 'seems in a sense to be living again the temptations of Christ: Ireland is being asked to prefer the "Kingdoms of this world with their splendour" to the kingdom of God (Mt 4:8). Satan, the tempter, the adversary of Christ, will use all his might and deceptions to win Ireland for the way of the world....Now is the time of testing for Ireland. This generation is once more a generation of decision....Dear sons and daughters of Ireland, pray, pray not to be led into temptation....I ask you for a great, intense and growing prayer for the....Church which owes so much to Ireland. Pray that Ireland may not fail in the test. Pray as Jesus taught us to pray. "Lead us not into temptation, but deliver us from evil."' A few years ago I also heard Cardinal Suenens speaking eloquently about the need for persistent prayer for the renewal and upbuilding of the Church. To support his point he quoted these relevant words from Isaiah 62:6-8, 'I have posted watchmen (i.e. intercessors) on your walls, Jerusalem (i.e. the Church), who shall not keep silence day or night: "You who invoke the Lord's name, take no rest, give him no rest until he makes Jerusalem a theme of endless praise on earth."'

11

Identifying and repairing the breaches

Besides defending ourselves and the Church from the attacks of the Evil One, the Lord is calling us to identify and to repair the breaches in our own lives and in the life of the Church. Again, there are many examples of this in the Bible and in Church history. For instance, in about 445BC Nehemiah heard that the walls and gates of Jerusalem had been virtually destroyed. When he asked his employer, Artaxerxes, King of Persia, for leave of absence, his request was granted. Nehemiah set out for Judah and surveyed the damage. Then he rallied the support of his countrymen with these stirring words: 'You see the trouble that we are in, how Jerusalem lies in ruins with its gates burned, Come, let us rebuild the walls of Jerusalem, so that we may no longer suffer disgrace' (Ne 2:17).

Many of the Jewish people rallied to the call, and began the apparently impossible task of restoring the city's defences. Each family set to work on the section of wall nearest its home. The workers were subjected to frequent attacks by their enemies, but Nehemiah encouraged them, saying, 'Do not be afraid of them. Remember the Lord, who is great and awesome, and fight for your kin' (Ne 4:14). At a practical level, he decided that, from then onwards, half of his followers would defend the breaches while the other half continued the task of reconstruction. Finally, despite lack of food and frequent bouts of exhaustion and disillusionment, the walls and gates of Jerusalem were restored. Afterwards, Nehemiah set about the task of restoring and renewing the religious life of the people.

There are echoes of this biblical account in the life of St Francis of Assisi. On one occasion he retired to the church of San Damiano, which was in a state of disrepair. There he prayed, 'Great and glorious God, my Lord Jesus Christ, I implore you to enlighten me and to disperse the darkness of my soul. Give me true faith and firm hope and a perfect charity. Grant me, O Lord, to know you so well that in all things I may act by your light, and in accordance with your holy will...Speak, Lord, for your servant is listening.' Then, one fateful day, he heard an inner voice saying to him, 'Now go forth, Francis, and build up my house, for it is nearly falling down!'[4] He took the words to heart and set about the task of restoring San Damiano. Later on he refurbished the churches of San Pietro and Portiuncula outside Assisi. All this activity was a prophetic sign, symbolising in deeds a need for spiritual restoration. For the rest of his life, Francis and his many followers worked tirelessly and effectively to bring about a renewal of the Christian Church.

Something similar is required today. Later I'll suggest some ways in which it can come about. Suffice it to say, at the moment, that committed Christians, especially those in positions of authority or responsibility, need to alert those people they came in contact with, in a humble but courageous way, about current dangers and infidelities, while summoning them to the all-important task of renewal and restoration. For example, I firmly believe that we should gently urge individuals and groups both to identify and to repair those breaches in their personal and collective lives that leave them vulnerable to the influence of 'the prince of this world' (Jn 12:31). In so far as they fail to do so, the Lord will have reason to say, 'I sought for anyone among them who would repair the wall and stand in the breach before me on behalf of the land...but I found no one' (Ezk 22:30). As Pope St Gregory the Great explained, 'To go up into the breaches means to withstand the powers of this world.'

A time of purification and preparation

It is my heartfelt conviction that the Lord has allowed the current affliction of the Church for a purpose. As scripture says, 'The Lord has led you...in the wilderness, in order to humble you, testing you to know what is in your heart' (Dt 8:2-3). Sometimes, like St Peter who promised so much, we find that although we may have had the desire to do what is right, we haven't always had the power to do so, due to our lack of spiritual maturity. While our sufferings and many failures reveal our worldliness, thank God that our subsequent repentance leads us away from secular values and beliefs to become more centred on Christ and his Gospel. In this way St Paul's advice is fulfilled: 'You must give up your old way of life, you must put aside your old self, which gets corrupted by following illusory desires. Your mind must be renewed by a spiritual revolution so that you can put on the new self that has been created in God's way' (Ep 4:22-23). It is only when we have have been purified, strengthened and renewed in this way by the Spirit, that the Lord will be able to use us to evangelise effectively in the future.

In the meantime it is vital that we become, in the words of Isaiah 58:12, 'breach-menders'. For only a renewed Church will have both the desire and the power to become God's answer to the cry of those who will seek him, especially during the time when secular society may be afflicted in various ways. (For more on this, see the end of chapter 7.) Then, and only then, will the prophecy spoken in the presence of Pope Paul VI on Easter Monday 1975 be fulfilled. We will participate in 'the greatest age of evangelisation the world has ever seen'.

2

UNDERSTANDING THE EXPERIENCE OF EVIL

From childhood onwards the eye of the heart is progressively opened to the reality of evil. It can begin with a fear of the imaginary ghouls, ghosts and monsters which are depicted in fairy tales, myths and legends. Later on we can be appalled by news of wars, famines, natural disasters, diseases and vicious crimes of every kind. This growing awareness of external evil may be matched by a dim recognition of the evil tendencies which lurk within our own breasts. But, as Carl Jung observed, 'it is quite within the bounds of possibility for a person to recognise the relative evil of his or her nature, but it is a rare and shattering experience for such a person to gaze into the face of absolute evil.' This fact has been confirmed by the findings of the Alister Hardy Research Centre at Oxford which investigates various types of religious experience. It has discovered that only a minority of people have reported a direct awareness of evil.

Encountering evil

When it does occur such an awareness can take place in an objective way. For example, a number of years ago I hitched a lift from Heidelberg to Munich. The driver happened to drop me off at the entrance of Dachau concentration camp. I decided to go inside. As I visited its museum, huts, gas chambers and crematoria, I was so overwhelmed by the enormity of the crime committed there, that instead of knowing about evil, as heretofore, I seemed to experience it directly. As I peered through that particular keyhole of perversity, I had a spine-chilling intimation of the darkness in the world. I felt as never before that there was a real force of iniquity which seemed to be more than the personification of human alienation and malice.

In recent times two crimes in particular have enabled many people in these islands to have a similar encounter with evil. The senseless murder of James Bulger by two young boys shocked

15

millions of people, not only in Britain, but in other countries as well. In Ireland where, sadly, we are all too familiar with murders and maimings, people were appalled and upset to an unusual degree by the killings in the West of Ireland of Imelda Rainey, her three- year-old son Liam, and local curate Fr Joe Walsh. These events seemed to penetrate the normal defence mechanisms which the unconscious mind uses to edit and filter the awareness of evil. As a result, many people have been traumatised by these and similar events. While it is good that counsellors have helped local people to cope with their subjective feelings of shock, grief, fear, anger etc., I hope that the following chapters will enable all of us to reflect in a constructive way on the irrationality and perversity of objective evil.

The evil we sense in the world about us, e.g. in Cambodia, Rwanda and Bosnia, can also be experienced within the personality. In Jeremiah 17:9-10 we read, 'The heart is more devious than any other thing, and is depraved; who can pierce its secrets?' Self-knowledge can grow in many ways. For example, in their book *Seeing the Invisible*, M. Maxwell and V. Tschudin recount how a woman was gently admonished by a male friend for the harsh way she had spoken to him. Afterwards his words had a profound effect. She said that her heart unravelled like a piece of knitting as she became aware, not of dramatic shortcomings, but of the unkindness, falsehood, hypocrisy, silliness and, finally, of the very locus of evil – her own heart. She says that she became conscious of the fact that all her customary kindness and decency was a desperate attempt to get away from this evil within herself, and that every one of her virtues had a flip-side of unspeakable nastiness. She asserted that 'this was not shown me as an abstract or intellectual idea: I was walking through a desolate swamp of stinking, stagnant water that I knew to be my own interior country.' She went on to say that she became aware that all the evil within her could be reduced to two forms, hate and greed. 'These huge paired monsters, Greed with her swollen belly, Hate with his jaws and pincers, were locked within me in totally unavailing battle.'[1]

The origin of evil
Once people have had a direct experience of evil, they face a problem

which has perplexed us since the beginning of recorded history; what is evil and where does it come from? While most religions and philosophies agree that evil exists, they differ greatly in their understanding of its nature and cure. For example, Zoroastrianism, a Persian religion founded by Mani in 215AD, adopted a dualistic point of view. Human beings were victims of evil because they were imprisoned in the material body with its perverted desires. Salvation would be experienced when the mind was illumined by right knowledge and all the passions and sexual appetites of the body were renounced. In Hinduism, good and evil are in a sense both illusions. While they are inevitable in this 'valley of tears' they have no place in Brahman or God. Salvation becomes possible when the person is freed from illusion, by overcoming egocentric concerns, desires and passions.

In the Jewish Old Testament, the understanding of evil evolved over the centuries. At first the Jews had an unrefined notion of divinity. Everything originated in God, including evil. For example, in Lamentations 3:36 we read, 'From where, if not from the mouth of the Most High, do evil and good come?' And again, in Isaiah 45:5-7, 'I am the Lord....I form the light and create darkness: I make peace and create evil.' Later, however, the Old Testament writers began to attribute evil to a powerful diabolical creature called Satan. In Hebrew his name means the 'adversary' or 'accuser'. He is the one who successfully tempted Adam and Eve to rebel against God. As a result they were driven out of paradise and became, like their descendants, subject to suffering and death. As Wisdom 2:24 attests, 'Death came into the world only through the Devil's envy.' Jesus inherited and, by and large, endorsed later Jewish beliefs about demonology. Speaking as an exorcist he said, 'If it is by the finger of God that I cast out demons, then the Kingdom of God has come to you' (Lk 11:20).

The Devil in modern thought
Until relatively recently most Christians would have accepted traditional teaching about the Devil's role in leading people into wrongdoing and evil. However since the Enlightenment and the rise of science, western thinking about the nature of evil has been changing. For example, in Germany, Ludwig Feuerbach (d. 1872)

suggested in *The Essence of Christianity* that God and the Devil were nothing but a projection of the human potential for good and evil. As a result he reinterpreted religious beliefs in purely human terms. He said, 'Man's God is man, this is the highest law of ethics. This is the turning point in world history.' Around the same time, Auguste Comte (d. 1857) argued in *Positive Philosophy* that history can be divided into three eras: the religious, up to 500BC; the philosophical, up to 1500AD; and the modern era of scientific positivism. He argued that religious and philosophical forms of knowledge had been rendered redundant by science. A study of subsequent intellectual history shows how these two men have had many followers, notably, Marx, Nietzsche and Freud. Because all of them rejected the notion of God and the devil, they advocated purely human solutions to the problem of evil.

Liberal and conservative responses

These rational and naturalistic approaches to suffering and evil have had quite an impact upon the Christian understanding of the Devil and his role. A recent European Values Systems Report[2] indicated that only twenty-five per cent of those surveyed believed in the existence of the Devil. In general, it could be said that there has been a growing dissolution of the supernatural as the central religious category. It has been replaced by a more secularised perspective. Not surprisingly, theologians have tried to respond to this paradigm shift. While most of them retain their belief in God and Christ, some have tried to strip the Old and New Testaments of their supernatural elements, such as belief in healings, miracles, visions, Satan and evil spirits. For example, Rudolf Bultmann has maintained that the world view, which is taken for granted in the preaching of Jesus and the New Testament, is generally mythological. When these mythological elements are sifted out, texts about the Devil are understood in terms of the evil that lurks in the human heart and inheres in the unjust and inhuman structures, beliefs and values of society.

Conservative theologians take a more moderate position. While they accept that there are mythological aspects in the Old and New Testaments, they try to get behind the images to see what essential truths they contain. So, while they would accept that references to the Devil, e.g. in Genesis and Revelation, are sometimes bizarre and culture-bound, they would believe – with certain qualifications – that the Devil does indeed exist. They would agree with Pope Paul VI when he said, 'It is a departure from the picture provided by biblical and Church teaching to refuse to acknowledge the Devil's existence...or to explain the Devil as a pseudo-reality, a conceptual and fanciful personification of the unknown causes of our misfortunes.'[3] Modern theologians believe that the Devil can exercise a malevolent influence on individuals and groups, and through them on the structures of society and vice versa. For example, some of them have described the way in which individual and group egoism can lead to what is called 'false consciousness'. In spite of apparent economic, cultural and military successes, it can lead entire nations, like Nazi Germany and the former Soviet Union, to increasing degrees of blindness, irrationality and irresponsibility. Such a declining culture can exercise an evil but sometimes unrecognised influence upon a person or group. Not surprisingly, the Devil can exploit circumstances like these for his own divisive and destructive purposes, all of which are alien to love.

Conclusion
French philosopher Paul Ricoeur talks about the need for a 'second *naiveté*', a return to basic beliefs by means of a painful process of intellectual and psychological purification. I think that this is not only possible, it is vitally important in the post-Newtonian age in which we live. We need to recover a sense of the supernatural, one that acknowledges, in a critical way, the existence and activity of good and bad spirits, including the Devil. For, unless we do, we will become by default the victims of him whose very existence we have denied. W. B. Yeats has described the probable results.

Things fall apart, the centre cannot hold;
Mere anarchy is loosed upon the world.
The blood-dimmed tide is loosed, and everywhere
The ceremony of innocence is drowned;
The best lack all conviction, while the worst
Are full of passionate intensity.[4]

3

MODERN SCIENCE AND THE DEVIL

On 18 January 1913 the famous Italian stigmatist, Padre Pio, wrote a letter to a colleague. It described one of the diabolical attacks he had recently endured. He said that the evil spirits had appeared to him, 'in the most abominable form'. When he refused to do their bidding, 'they hurled themselves upon me, threw me to the floor, struck me violently, threw pillows, books and chairs through the air and cursed me with exceedingly filthy words.'[1]

About two years ago, a BBC local radio station sent me a tape. I was asked to comment on an unusual case involving a four-year-old girl who was regularly disturbed by a man who used to appear to her in her bedroom. It was alleged that these apparitions were associated with things like a drop in room temperature and the spontaneous combustion of plaster cast statues which failed to leave any burn marks on the wooden mantelpiece. A baby brother who was in the same room was found to have bruising on his body, although there was no evidence that he had been touched by anyone. When consulted about these occurrences, local priests either dismissed them out of hand, or were at a loss as to what to do. Finally, the family left the house and their spooky problems ended immediately.

The way in which one interprets such strange accounts is largely determined by one's world-view. Such a framework is made up of a set of basic assumptions, conscious and unconscious, about the nature of reality. It determines how people will evaluate any experience and what they will accept or reject. At present, there are two basic world-views operating in western countries.

The secular world-view
Firstly, there is the predominating outlook which understands reality in a materialistic and rationalistic way. It maintains that we live in a purely physical world, one which can be understood in exclusively scientific terms. Any notion of a non-physical, spiritual

realm is considered to be an illusion. For example, Freud believed that religion was a form of collective obsessional neurosis, an escape from the harsh reality of everyday life into a make-believe world of fanciful beliefs. 'Psychoanalysis,' he wrote, 'has made us familiar with the intimate connection between the father complex and belief in God; it is nothing other than an exalted father...thus we recognise that the roots of the need for religion are in the paternal complex.'[2]

This world-view would interpret the strange events mentioned above in a reductionist way, e.g. as nothing but schizophrenic episodes. For instance, in the *Diagnostic and Statistical Manual of Mental Disorders* (DSM-3-R) which is used by American psychiatrists, schizophrenia is described as 'odd or bizarre ideation, or magical thinking'. Later on it says that the illness involves unusual experiences, e.g. 'recurrent illusions, sensing the presence of a force or person not actually present'. Not surprisingly, therefore, it states that the beliefs or experiences of many religious people 'may be difficult to distinguish from delusions or hallucinations'. So, not only would this world-view discount the validity of any demonic experience, it would be sceptical about all types of religious awareness.

The religious world-view

There is a second world-view, which maintains that besides the physical world there is also the non-physical realm of spiritual reality. It is experienced intuitively in largely non-rational ways, by means of prophecy, dreams, visions, mystical experiences etc. This perspective can be traced back to people like Plato and Jesus, and has been advocated by thinkers such as Augustine, Aquinas and Jung. Indeed, unlike Freud, who thought that religious experience was a form of neurosis, Jung maintained that neurosis was probable without it. 'In 30 years,' he wrote, 'I have treated many patients in the second half of life, i.e. over 35 years of age. Everyone of them fell ill because they had lost that which the living religions in every age have given their followers, and none of them was fully healed who did not regain his or her religious outlook.'[3]

Those who adopt a religious world-view are more inclined to

accept the possibility of affliction by evil spirits. While they would admit that in many instances these states can be understood in purely psychological terms, there are others which are not amenable to such an explanation. On rare occasions, evil spirits can impinge upon human experience with all kinds of strange effects. For example, in *People of the Lie*, psychiatrist M. Scott Peck recounts how he observed two exorcisms. He said that as a hard-headed scientist he could explain ninety-five per cent of what went on in terms of psychological dynamics, but the other five per cent could only be accounted for by believing that it was due to the influence of evil spirits.[4]

A new world-view

Recently, some authors have explored the relationship of science and religion. They have shown that, whereas post-Newtonian physics was antagonistic to religion, modern science has abandoned some of its materialistic and rationalistic assumptions. For example, a growing number of scientists wonder whether, strictly speaking, matter exists at all. It seems to be a manifestation of energy. Sometimes it seems to behave like self-thinking thought! And instead of relying on reason alone, some eminent scientists have relied on their intuition, emotions and aesthetic sense when formulating new theories. For example, Einstein has revealed that he worked out his ideas about relativity in this way. Only later did he express and defend them in rational, mathematical terms. He once wrote, 'The most beautiful and most profound emotion we can experience is the sensation of the mystical. It is the source of all true science.'[5]

The paranormal and non-physical reality

I have long believed that paranormal experiences are important because they lie at the mid-point between physical and non-physical reality. If modern science could establish the legitimacy of paranormal experiences, it could go on to challenge an exclusively materialistic world-view. By doing so, it would open the door to a more open-minded recognition of the spiritual dimension of life. This might include, among other things, the reality and activity of evil spirits. The late Sir Alister Hardy, an eminent scientist who was interested in religious experience, maintained that if there was scientific evidence for the existence of extra-sensory perception, it could have important implications. 'I believe,' he wrote, in *The Spiritual Nature of Man*, 'that it would help people to accept a spiritual philosophy which is greatly needed in our materialistic society; it would show that there was a mental extension of the individual's psyche beyond the physico-chemical structure of the brain and so would lend plausibility to the concept of there being a spiritual dimension outside that of the strictly physical, material world.'[6]

For example, in October 1977, I had a strange premonition. As I was walking from one classroom to another in a school in Northern Ireland, I had a sudden and spontaneous conviction that Charlie Chaplin would die on Christmas day of that year. I was so certain of this, that I told a colleague about my prediction, so that following its fulfilment, he would be able to verify that I had told him about it beforehand. Because I believed that God had revealed this information for a purpose, I asked a local prayer group to pray that the famous comic would die in a happy and peaceful way. On Christmas morning, the first thing I heard on the radio was the news that Sir Charles Chaplin had died unexpectedly some hours before, at 3.00a.m.

The secular, Newtonian world-view would have dismissed such a prediction either as a matter of coincidence or as sign of mental instability. However, modern science is a little more open-minded. In the fifties, Jung came up with the complicated notion of 'synchronicity'. He argued that a premonition could be accounted for if the usual notion of cause and effect were abandoned in favour of an a-causal connecting principle. He believed that the world was like a giant telephone exchange where everybody and everything was linked by means of its overall unity. He felt that, on rare occasions, intuitive people could eavesdrop on a call, without the usual constraints of space and time. In this way they could have access to information about a person or future event, without using their five senses.

Around the same period, quantum physicists predicted that particles could respond to one another, from a great distance, without being influenced by the cause and effect relationship which was taken for granted in Newtonian physics. This would imply that they were being affected by the a-causal connecting principle that Jung had spoken about. On 20 February 1983, the *Sunday Times* reported that experimental verification of the prediction made by quantum physicists had taken place. More recently, Michael Talbot has suggested[7] that accurate premonitions show that reality is a giant holograph where the whole world is present in each of its parts, e.g. via the unconscious mind of the clairvoyant person. It seems that the Hippocratics of ancient Greece were correct when they wrote, 'there is one common flow, one common breathing, all things are in sympathy'.

Depth psychology and demons

It would appear, therefore, that the Newtonian world-view is being replaced by a less materialistic one. There is a growing compatibility between scientific and religious ways of knowing. As a science, depth psychology will have an increasingly important role to play in reconciling the two. For example, Jung not only tried to explain how premonitions could occur; like Plato he also tried to understand how nonphysical reality relates to the human psyche. He thought that the pre-rational dimensions of the unconscious were an important contact point between human experience and the spiritual realm of good and bad spirits, etc.

He explored how the Devil could act upon the human personality through the workings of the psyche, its powers and its pathologies. It is probable that Satan and his demons do this firstly by exploiting the negative aspects of what sociologists refer to as the 'anonymous powers and systems' of society. They would include such things as class divisions, inequalities, injustices and prejudices of all sorts. Secondly, these can impinge in a negative way on the darker, shadowy aspects of the unconscious mind, such as unacknowledged feelings of inferiority, alienation, resentment etc. In other words, the experience of evil may be the outcome of a subtle interrelationship of personal and social factors, which can be exploited by the Devil.

Robert Waite[8] and Alice Miller[9] have shown how this can happen, in their insightful biographies of Hitler. They are chilling psychological studies of how a person who grew up in a troubled society and was hurt and abused as a child, could become one of the arch-destroyers of the twentieth century. As we reach the second millennium, the secular world-view which has prevailed in our century with such disastrous results, is being modified at last. This is just as well, because if we don't learn from history, we are destined to repeat it. We will do better in the future if we abandon the soul-destroying limitations of a materialistic world-view that ignores the nature and dynamics of diabolical evil.

4

TO THE DEVIL WITH PSYCHOLOGY

For years, Robert Louis Stephenson looked for a story that would convey his 'strong sense of men's double being'. Eventually the plot of Dr Jekyll and Mr Hyde was revealed to him in a dream and the famous novel was published in 1885. It explored a man's schizophrenic identity, one side good, the other evil. It was a brilliant illustration of the adage that at the heart of the human problem is the problem of the human heart.

Many psychologists have explored this theme. Jung believed that what drives people to war with themselves is the suspicion that they consist of two persons in opposition to one another. The conflict can arise between the sensual and the spiritual self, or between the ego and the shadow. It is what Faust meant when he said: 'Two souls, alas, are housed within my breast.' A neurosis, according to Jung, was a splitting of personality, the state of being at war with oneself.

Psychologist Rollo May has pointed out that this civil war of the heart is 'diabolical' from a psychological point of view. Our English word is derived from the Greek which literally means 'to tear apart'. So when a person is subject to irrational inner conflicts, it is a diabolic emotional experience. Human alienation can also also be 'diabolical,' from a spiritual point of view. It tends to render its victims more susceptible to temptation. The devil can exploit their vulnerability and thereby lead them into wrongdoing. When they indulge their negative impulses and desires they can suffer from a sense of anxiety, and guilt. Then Satan, 'the accuser,' can exploit this awareness of failure by filling the person with a feeling of self-condemnation. This only serves to widen and deepen the split between the acceptable and unacceptable self.

Freud's views on the Devil
Working within the constraints of a secular world-view, Freud rejected the religious interpretation of evil. He maintained that in order to satisfy the sometimes overweening demands of a moral-

istic conscience, people had to repress the insistent urges of their pleasure-seeking, human instincts. He believed that it was this repressed material which was projected outwards and personified as the Devil. He wrote: 'The neuroses of olden times were masquerading in demonical shape and evil spirits were the projection of base and evil wishes into the world.' On another occasion he said 'the Devil is certainly nothing else than the personification of the repressed instinctual life.'[1] This statement is at once dogmatic and reductionist. It makes an unjustifiable jump from a psychological description of subjective reality to an emphatic philosophical conclusion about the objective state of things.

Ironically, many religious people have accepted Freud's questionable critique of demonology while retaining their belief in God. He would have been the first to point out the logical inconsistency of such an approach. From a psychological point of view God and the Devil are two sides of the same coin. If one accepts the concept of the Devil as nothing but a psychological projection of unconscious elements in the personality, so too, by implication, is the concept of God.

Jung on the shadow

As a depth psychologist Jung explained the experience of evil in terms of what he called the shadow. This term referred to the neglected, unwanted side of the personality. One image of the shadow is that of a retarded relative. Years ago families who were ashamed of a mentally handicapped son or daughter might lock the child in a back room, out of sight. While that inhuman practice seems to be a thing of the past, we still do it to ourselves. Whenever the darker, weaker side of our nature is experienced, we reject it. Any feeling or desire which we find hard to face is buried alive in the wells of the unconscious. From there it poisons the waters of our conscious feelings, thoughts and attitudes.

Jung argued that this form of repression reveals itself in our tendency to project our shadow on to other people and groups. We see and condemn in them, the very weaknesses and tendencies we have failed to acknowledge or to accept in ourselves. Surely this dynamic explains a lot of the conflict in marriage, family life and the workplace. Social groups can also project the contents of their collective shadow on to some minority in their midst. For example, the Nazis believed in Aryan superiority, so they made the Jews the carriers of their collective shadow. Hitler wrote: 'The Jews eat like poisonous abscesses into the nation....We will not pause until the last trace of this poison is removed from the body of our people.'[2]

If the Jews were thought to be contaminated, then in a perverse way, 'the final solution' seemed to be at the service of life. Most killing is not done out of sadism, not even Nazi killing. The murders are motivated by a perverted vision of life enhancement. As Arthur Koestler once observed,[3] the number of violent crimes committed for consciously base motives fades into insignificance compared to those committed for idealistic motives, i.e. out of self-sacrificing devotion to a flag, a leader, a religious faith, or a political cause.

The evil involved in all types of armed conflict can be understood in terms of the activity of the shadow. As Jung observed in 1928, 'The psychology of war is a matter of unconscious projection. Everything our own nation does is good, everything which the other nation does is wicked. The centre of all that is mean and vile is always to be found several miles behind the enemy's lines.' As we have seen in Yugoslavia, Northern Ireland and many other trouble spots, once the enemy has been demonised, killing and destruction can be justified as good and necessary things.

Jung on complexes

Besides the shadow, Jung also spoke about the role of 'complexes'. They consist of unconscious feelings, thoughts and memories that cluster together to form an independent and powerful 'mini-personality' within the psyche. He thought that negative complexes, e.g. of an aggressive or abusive kind, could possess people from within, and lead them to commit all kinds of foul and irrational deeds. Afterwards they might truthfully say, 'I don't know what came over me.... It wasn't like me to act like that', etc. Indeed, in his early years, Jung sometimes wondered whether the notion of the complexes 'might not be a description of primitive demonology'.

The Devil and the psyche

At this point a question arises. Did Jung believe that there was a Devil? Like Freud, he thought that the notions of God and the Devil were inextricably linked from a psychological point of view. Unlike Freud, however, he seemed to believe that both God and the Devil existed in fact. He avoided the danger of reductionism by acknowledging the existence of a non-physical realm that included good and bad spirits. He felt that they could impinge upon the personality by influencing the negative complexes and the darker side of the shadow self. In a letter to Bill Wilson, the founder of Alcoholics Anonymous, Jung wrote: 'I am strongly convinced that...an ordinary person unprotected by an action from above and isolated in society, cannot resist the power of evil, which is very aptly called the Devil.' At the end of World War II, in a psychological study of the Nazi phenomenon, he observed that 'just when people were congratulating themselves on having abolished evil spirits, it turned out that instead of haunting the attic or old ruins, the spirits were flitting about in the heads of apparently normal Europeans. Tyrannical, obsessive, intoxicating ideas and delusions were abroad everywhere, and people began to believe the most absurd things, just as the possessed do.'[4]

Overcoming evil

On the basis of his analysis of evil, Jung was able to make perceptive suggestions about different means of overcoming it. His advice could be summed up in two phrases. Firstly, 'accept and love yourself as you are', and secondly, 'in your struggle with evil, rely on the power of God to help you'. We will look at each point in turn.

In *Psychology and Western Religion* Jung wrote these famous words: 'Acceptance of oneself is the essence of the moral problem...That I feed a beggar, that I forgive an insult, that I love my enemy in the name of Christ – all these are undoubtedly great virtues. What I do for the least of my brothers and sisters, that I do unto Christ. But what if I should discover that the least among them all, the poorest of all the beggars, the most impudent of all the offenders, yes the very fiend himself – that these are within me, and that I myself stand in need of the alms of my own kindness, that I myself am the enemy who must be loved?'[5] Jung says that if we want to be delivered from evil, we need to withdraw our negative projections from other people and groups. Then we need consciously to acknowledge their origin within our own psyches.

Jung would have agreed that Steps Four and Five of Alcoholics Anonymous would help alienated people to grow in self-awareness and self-acceptance. They could begin by making a list of the wrongs they had committed themselves and the wrongs they had endured at the hands of others. After that, they would need courage to admit these things to themselves, to God and to another human being. He felt that if people could tell the unvarnished truth about themselves to a non-judgemental confidant or friend, a great inner healing could take place. As they sensed the acceptance and love of the other person, they would begin to accept and love themselves, as they are, warts and all. As Dr Jekyll and Mr Hyde are reconciled within, they are progressively delivered from the self-hatred which is the source of many evils. As St Paul wrote: 'The commandments, "You shall not commit adultery; you shall not murder; You shall not steal; You shall not covet; and any other commandment, are summed up in this word, 'Love your neighbour as yourself" ' (Rm 13:9-11).

While self-acceptance fosters psychological and spiritual growth, Jung recognised that the capacity to commit evil remains latent within us. As a result, he believed that we could only overcome temptation and wrongdoing if we relied on the word and the power of God. He wrote: 'Freud has unfortunately overlooked the fact that man has never yet been able single-handed to hold his own against the powers of darkness....He has always stood in need of spiritual help...He is never helped in his suffering by what he thinks of for himself: only superhuman, revealed truth lifts him out of distress.'[6] Most of the remaining chapters of this book will be devoted to spelling out the implications of this statement.

5

DOES THE DEVIL EXIST?

In the preceding chapters we saw that there are divided views about the existence of Satan. On the one hand, people who espouse a scientific world-view, e.g. Freud, tend to accept the psychological argument that the Devil is merely a projection of the darker side of the human mind. For them, he is simply a personification, a symbol for the experience of evil. On the other hand, those who espouse a religious world-view tend to accept the traditional Christian belief that the Devil is an angelic creature, perverted and perverting, who exercises a malign but often hidden influence on human affairs. In recent times, however, the two points of view have begun to overlap in a paradoxical way. Nowadays, followers of a holistic, scientific world-view, e.g. Jung, Bohm, Capra etc., are open to the reality of a spiritual realm which includes good and bad spirits. At the same time, there are many Christians who have been influenced by secular thinking, e.g. Bultmann, who accept doctrines such as the divinity of Christ, while rejecting the existence of the Devil. In this chapter I will try to answer the question, Does the Church teach in an authoritative way that the Devil exists? Besides looking at its official pronouncements and its liturgy, I will take a brief look at what some eminent scripture scholars, theologians and spiritual writers have had to say on the subject.

The Devil in the scriptures
Whereas the Devil was hardly ever mentioned in the Old Testament, he is mentioned time and time again in the New Testament. Indeed, Morton Kelsey says that there are seventy-five references to the Devil and 128 references to demons in the four gospels and the Acts of the Apostles.[1] Joachim Jeremias has pointed out that in the Judaism of Jesus' time, the demons were seen predominantly as unorganised individual beings, haphazardly inclined to inflict physical, psychological and moral evils. He saw Satan, the one and only Devil, as 'Prince of this world'

(Jn 12:31), the ruler and commander (Lk 10:19) of an organised army of demons who could afflict the human race with sin, disease and death. From the beginning to the very end of his public ministry, the evangelists depict the saving activity of Jesus as a fight against the powers of darkness. He sometimes spoke in his parables about the enemy of God and his people. He discerned that the Evil One was oppressing and possessing some people, and causing the mental and physical illnesses of others. As St Peter said of him, 'You have heard how God anointed Jesus of Nazareth with the Holy Spirit and power; how he went about doing good and healing all that were oppressed by the Devil, for God was with him' (Ac 10:38).

How should we interpret all these references to the Devil and demons? Are they merely mythological personifications of human sin and evil, as Bultmann suggests? We saw in chapter 2 that the answer depends on the world-view that informs the scholar's understanding of the scripture texts. If it excludes the existence of a non-physical realm of spiritual reality, it is inevitable that references to the Devil will be interpreted in a metaphorical rather than a literal way. Commenting on this reductionist approach, John P. Meier, a respected US scripture scholar, has stated[2] that such interpretations are based not on historical exegesis, but on a philosophical assumption about the nature of spiritual reality, an assumption rarely, if ever, defended with rigorous logic. Instead there are references to 'modern man', but he happens to look suspiciously like eighteenth-century Enlightenment man. If, on the other hand, scripture scholars believe in the existence of a non-physical realm of spiritual reality, they will, with certain qualifications, affirm the existence of the Devil. For example, Raymond Brown is one of the most distinguished Catholic biblical scholars writing in English. In two of his recent books, *Responses to 101 Questions on the Bible*[3] and *An Introduction to New Testament Christology*,[4] he clearly states that he believes that the Devil exists and that Jesus was an exorcist. James Dunn, the well-known British scripture scholar, makes much the same point. In his book, *Jesus and the Spirit*,[5] he states that the gospel references to the healing of demon-possessed people are historically reliable. Apparently there have been no developments in recent scripture scholarship which would give reason to question this judgement. On the contrary, they have reinforced the essential historicity and importance of Jesus' work as an exorcist.

It is worth noting that in Jesus' own day there was divided opinion about the existence or non-existence of the Devil and clean and unclean spirits. The Pharisees accepted the common inter-testamental belief in the existence of both. The Saducees, in contrast, rejected both belief in the resurrection of the dead, and in the existence of good or evil spirits. It is significant that Jesus chose to adopt the prevailing view as his own. As one document, *Christian Faith and Demonology*, says, 'To maintain today, that the words of Jesus express only a teaching borrowed from his culture and are unimportant for the faith of other believers shows little understanding either of the Master's character or of his age.'[6]

The Devil in modern theology

The differing views of scripture scholars about the existence of the Devil are also reflected by theologians. For example, a number of years ago the theologian Henry Kelly wrote a book entitled *The Devil, Demonology and Witchcraft*,[7] in which he argued that belief in the Devil's existence was not only unnecessary but harmful. It is an unnecessary theological hypothesis, because belief in the Devil's existence is assumed rather than affirmed in the scriptures and in Church teaching. In the light of modern knowledge this particular belief is neither necessary or helpful as a means of understanding the nature and dynamics of evil. It is a harmful belief in so far as it has encouraged fundamentalist and superstitious attitudes of mind which have sometimes resulted in fanaticism and cruelty like the burning of so-called witches in the Middle Ages and later. Hans Küng agrees with this latter point when he writes: 'Herbert Haag has rightly bade good-bye to personified evil and belief in the Devil, both of which have done untold harm.'[8] Küng seems to interpret the concept of the Devil in purely sociological terms when he writes: 'Certainly the power of evil, as it finds expression in the life and death of Jesus, should not be minimised even today....In the light of both the

New Testament (i.e. principalities and powers) and of modern sociological conclusions (i.e. anonymous powers and systems), evil as power is essentially more than the sum total of the wickedness of individuals.'[9] What he seems to imply in this quotation is the rather Marxist belief that the evil which impinges on people's lives is institutionalised in the corrupt and unjust attitudes and structures of culture and society.

There are many theologians who do assert that the Devil exists. In *Signs and Wonders*, Louis Monden maintains that to read the scriptures with an open mind, without preconceived ideas, makes it clear that one cannot do away with the Devil as a personal entity without changing the Christian message in its very essence. Morton Kelsey and Victor White, both of whom are theologians with an interest in depth psychology, agree with this view. Karl Rahner was perhaps the greatest Catholic theologian of the century. Speaking about the existence of the Devil he wrote: 'The existence of angels cannot be disputed in the view of the conciliar declarations. Consequently it will be firmly maintained that the existence of angels and demons is affirmed in Scripture and not merely assumed as a hypothesis which we can drop today.'[10] While Rahner accepted that the Devil exists, he would have been the first to warn against the dangers of a simplistic fundamentalism. He would have advocated a critical understanding of demonology, one that got rid of unnecessary elements of a mythological nature.

The Devil in spiritual theology

As we shall see in chapters on temptation and the discernment of spirits, the existence and activity of the Devil has always been acknowledged in Christian spirituality. Over the centuries great spiritual writers have suggested guidelines which would help their disciples to discern when and how evil spirits might be at work. For example, in his *Christian Mysticism*,[11] Harvey Egan describes the bizarre effects of diabolical obsession and possession. Jordan Aumann[12] deals with the same subjects in an insightful and helpful way. He lists a number of the characteristics of a diabolical influence, such as a spirit of falsity, morbid curiosity, confusion, anxiety, deep depression, obstinacy, constant indiscretion, restlessness, pride, vanity, false humility, despair, disobedience, uncontrolled passions, hypocrisy etc. Aumann also describes the preternatural things the Devil can do, e.g. produce visions, false ecstasy, rays of light, inner consolation, the stigmata, simulated miracles, the disappearance of objects etc. While they accept the possibility of these things, contemporary spiritual writers warn their readers against naivety and credulity. They point out that the findings of psychiatrists and depth psychologists about the powers of the psyche need to be kept in mind, when making judgements about supposedly demonic phenomena.

The Devil in Church teaching

Theologians rightly argue that there is a hierarchy of truths in the Catholic Church. First order truths are contained in the creeds. While the Church teaches that the Devil exists, this would be an important but second order truth. Clearly it is not as important as the doctrines of the Trinity, the divinity of Christ, or justification through faith. That said, however, 1 John 3:8 states that the reason the Son of God appeared was to destroy the works of the Devil. Surely that is an important and relevant truth.

With these points in mind it is interesting to see what the new *Catechism of the Catholic Church* has to say about the existence of the Devil. Paragraphs 391-395 deal with the fallen angels. The first of them says, 'Behind the disobedient choice of our first parents lurks a seductive voice, opposed to God, which makes them fall into death out of envy. Scripture and the Church's tradition see in this being a fallen angel, called "Satan" or the "Devil". The Church teaches that Satan was at first a good angel, made by God: "The Devil and the other demons were indeed created naturally good by God, and they became evil by their own doing".' The last line in this quote is taken from the teaching of the Fourth Lateran Council which took place in 1215AD. It is the clearest and most authoritative statement of the Church's belief about the Devil. Nevertheless, theologians have divided opinions about it.

On the one hand there are those, such as Kelly and Schoonenberg, who argue that the reference to the Devil is only incidental in that conciliar decree. 'Even this doctrinal statement,' says Schoonenberg, 'which most explicitly speaks of angels and devils, presupposes but does not directly affirm their existence.'[13] On the other hand there are those who challenge the legitimacy of this approach. In a very carefully researched and closely argued article, Jesuit theologian Paul Qual concludes that 'doubts or denials that the existence of angels or devils is an article of Catholic faith has been shown to be without serious grounding. There is no way to restrict the defining intent of the Fourth Lateran Council merely to the universality and unity of God's creative activity and the creaturely origins of evil.'[14]

This view was confirmed in *Christian Faith and Demonology*,[15] published in Rome in 1975. It explains why the existence of Satan and the demons has never been the object of an explicit affirmation by the teaching authority of the Church: 'This is because the question has never been put in those terms. On the basis of scripture, heretics and the faithful alike were in agreement on the existence and chief misdeeds of Satan and his demons.' The same document concludes: 'We repeat, therefore, that, though still emphasising in our day the real existence of the demonic, the Church has no intention...of proposing an alternative explanation which would be more acceptable to reason. Its desire is simply to remain faithful to the Gospel and its requirements.' (sec. VII)

The Devil and liturgical texts

The Church's belief is reflected in a nuanced and balanced way in the liturgy, e.g. in the new rite of baptism. This isn't surprising really, because according to the traditional understanding which has its roots in the New Testament, to be baptised is to be freed from Satan's power. The first thing that is noticeable in the new rite is that the exorcisms which were used in the older ceremony have been dropped in favour of prayers of petition and invocation. We can look at one example. In the old rite the minister of the sacrament would address the Evil One and say, 'I exorcise you unclean spirit, by the Father, and the Son, and the Holy Spirit. Come forth and depart from these servants of God. For he commands you, accursed and damned one, he who opened the eyes of the man born blind and raised Lazarus from the tomb after four days.' In the new rite, the minister prays to the Lord saying, 'God of eternal life, who are God, not of the dead but of the living, and have sent your Son as a herald to snatch mankind from the realm of death and lead them to the resurrection; we pray that you will free these elect persons from the deadly power of the malign spirit, so that they may receive and testify to the new life of the Risen Christ. Amen.'

As Balthasar Fischer has noted in an article entitled 'Baptismal Exorcism in the Catholic Baptismal Rites after Vatican II',[16] because of a more refined and nuanced theology, we no longer speak to the Devil who is present; rather we speak to God about the presence of the Devil. As Fischer observes, while the new rite reflects the Church's traditional belief in the existence of the Devil, it avoids archaic and off-putting exorcisms on the one hand, and reductionist, wishy-washy prayers on the other.

Perhaps it would be appropriate to end this chapter with the renewal of baptismal promises which is still made by the parents and godparents in the new rite.

Celebrant:	Do you reject Satan?
Parents and godparents:	I do.
Celebrant:	And all his works?
Parents and godparents:	I do.
Celebrant:	And all his empty promises?
Parents and godparents:	I do.

6

POSSESSION AND EXORCISM EXPLAINED

Very few people have direct experience of either diabolical possession or exorcism. But these bizarre subjects have always fascinated film makers and their audiences. Movies tend to depict these phenomena in lurid and sensational ways. For example, in *The Exorcist* a demonised girl named Regan is endowed with preternatural powers. She is able to produce off-putting lesions, bloating, improbable neck turnings, cold spells, and extraordinary physical strength. Not only that, she is capable of levitating, knowing private events, speaking English backwards etc. As most people's notion of possession and exorcism depends on what they have seen in the cinema or on video, the question arises whether it is true to reality or inaccurate and misleading?

The Exorcist itself is an interesting case in point. The film was based on William Blatty's novel of the same name, which was, in turn, based on a case involving a fourteen-year-old boy from St Louis, Missouri, who was exorcised by a Jesuit priest named William Bodern in 1949. The first thing to note is that, whereas the book proposes the arguments for and against the reality of the child's possession, the film removes all doubt by answering the question in the affirmative. Secondly, Blatty's book is not really true to Fr Bodern's account. It collates the recorded characteristics of many exorcisms, and uses them to describe the Regan case. But, in reality, the boy in St Louis had been associated with poltergeist phenomena, i.e. unexplained noises, coats flying through the air, furniture moving about, etc.

At first a doctor was asked to examine the teenager. After he had done so, he declared that he was quite normal. Some time later, help was sought from the local Catholic Archbishop, Ritter. He asked Fr Bodern to perform an exorcism. As soon as it began, the troubled adolescent started to have violent convulsions and to experience spells of unconsciousness. The process of exorcism went on for thirty-five days. During all that time, the boy did not demonstrate any of the preternatural powers depicted in *The Exorcist.* The only striking phenomenon was the sudden appearance on his body of red welts resembling claw marks. On one occasion the word HELL appeared on his skin and faded in half an hour. Happily, after his final session with Fr Bodern, the boy returned to normal and remained so ever afterwards.

It is clear that the depiction of possession and exorcism in *The Exorcist* was true neither to Blatty's novel, nor to the real life account, upon which both were based. Indeed, it is questionable whether the boy Fr Bodern prayed for was really possessed. It is important to note that in Christian theology a distinction is made between diabolical possession and diabolical oppression.

Possession and oppression

Possession is a kind of spiritual psychosis. When people are possessed their entire personalities seem to be subject to demonic influence, and they often have preternatural powers, e.g. the ability to speak, or to understand strange languages. To be freed from their bondage, a solemn exorcism needs to be administered by an exorcist who has been officially appointed for that purpose by a local bishop.[1]

Oppression is a kind of spiritual neurosis. When people are oppressed, only part of their personalities seem to be subject to demonic influence. They may have unusual powers, but they retain some ability to make free choices. To be freed from the influence of an evil spirit, oppressed people need a prayer for deliverance which can be performed by any faith-filled Christian.

Possession assessed

While the Christian Church believes that possession is possible in theory, it maintains that it is very uncommon in practice. For example, Fr Joseph de Tonquedoc was the official Catholic exorcist in Paris for twenty years. In all that time, he was never convinced that he had come across a single case of genuine possession. Psychiatrists have shown that many of the strange powers and behaviours associated with possession can be explained in purely psychological terms.

In the nineteenth century Dr Jean Charcot was able to reproduce the symptoms of possession in hysterical type patients by the use of hypnosis. Other researchers maintain that even without hypnosis people who experience unusual mental states, and begin to believe that they are demon-possessed, may act in ways that they imagine to be consistent with demon-possession. This can easily happen if a fundamentalist Christian ignores the findings of psychology and mistakenly prays that a person with an emotional problem might be freed from the influence of an evil spirit. Exorcism is an impressive ceremony, capable of acting effectively on the unconscious of an impressionable person. The commands addressed to the demon, and perhaps sprinklings with holy water, repeated signs of the cross etc., can easily conjure up a diabolical fantasy from the unconscious of a vulnerable man or woman. 'Address the Devil,' says Fr de Tonqedoc, 'and you'll see him; or rather, not him, but a portrait made up of the sick person's ideas of him.'[2]

I witnessed this dynamic in action at a recent conference. The principal speaker seemed to have a naive and uncritical belief in the existence and activity of the Devil. He often spoke about the Evil One, and warned the people to be on their guard lest they fall under his influence. It struck me more than once that he may have had many unresolved emotional problems of his own. I also suspected that he was projecting personified aspects of his own unacknowledged shadow on to the people. Not surprisingly, those who were at risk from a psychological point of view accepted the transference. As the preacher spoke, some of them fell to the floor writhing, screaming and foaming at the mouth like people possessed. Then, having created this outbreak of religious hysteria – and I'm sure that's all it was – the preacher prayed that they might be delivered from the power of the Devil. In other words, he was creating the very problem that he was presuming to solve. In instances like these, religion is pathological, a sickness that mistakes itself for a cure.

Psychiatrists would maintain that the preternatural powers exercised by some apparently demon-possessed people can be explained in psychological terms. A case in point would be the welt marks and words that were seen on the body of the boy in St Louis. Roderick Gorney, an associate professor of psychiatry in Los Angeles, has produced single words, phrases, and even entire sentences on the bodies of subjects, by means of hypnotic suggestion. So, when all the evidence is assessed, it is not surprising that Professor Van Roo of the Gregorian University in Rome has said that nothing happened during the exorcism performed by William Bodern which would justify an emphatic claim that the boy was possessed. In all likelihood he was being *oppressed*, rather than *possessed*, by an evil spirit.[3]

Demonic oppression

There are many possible causes of spiritual oppression. Here are just three of them.

Firstly, some people have suffered traumatic hurts in the past, perhaps being sexually abused, abandoned, or cursed as a child, or having been the victim of an act of violence in adult life, e.g. being held as a hostage or raped. Incidents like these can leave terrible psychological scars. Occasionally, it seems as if the evil spirit exploits hurts like these to oppress people in some way or other.

Secondly, if people consent to serious and repeated wrong-doing, a pattern is created which can leave them vulnerable to the influence of the evil spirit in that area of their lives. I have met adults who were involved in deviant behaviour e.g. sex with animals, incestuous relationships, substance abuse, continued acts of violence as members of terrorist organisations, etc. As a result, they not only became addicted to the harmful behaviour, some of them seemed to become oppressed by an evil spirit.

Thirdly, involvement in the occult for whatever reason, e.g. fortune-telling, palmistry, astrology, black-magic, witchcraft, use of a ouija board, attempting to contact the dead etc., can lead some people to become oppressed by an evil spirit.

Prayer for deliverance

Once it has been discerned that a person may be spiritually oppressed by an evil influence, he or she can be set free by a prayer for deliverance. As Jesus promised in Mark 16:17, 'these are the signs that will be associated with believers: in my name they will cast out devils.' A prayer for deliverance is unlike a solemn exorcism, where the officially appointed exorcist asks God to order the evil spirit to depart from the victim's life. With expectant faith, the prayer asks God to deliver the person from any malign influence that might be impinging on his or her personality. The petition echoes the prayer which is said during the baptismal rite: 'Almighty God,...we pray for this person who has to face the world with its temptations and fight the Devil in all his cunning. Your Son died and rose again to save us. By this victory over sin and death, bring this person out of the power of darkness. Strengthen him/her with the grace of Christ, and watch over him/her at every step of life's journey.'

I was interested to see that in a biography of her friend St Francis de Sales, St Jane de Chantal wrote: 'About ten years before his death, and for a period of about two years, possessed people were very often brought to him – or at least they thought they were possessed – and when they left him they were healed or gently comforted. When I heard the talk about these "possessed" people, I asked the Blessed to tell me what was happening, and with great humility and modesty, he said,: "These people are good souls, who are suffering from some kind of *depression* (my italics). I hear their confession, give them Communion, comfort them as best I can and tell them they are cured; they believe what I say and go their way in peace." I have heard that hundreds of people afflicted like this were cured.'[4] This is a very interesting testimony from a number of points of view.

1. St Francis de Sales never met a person who needed solemn exorcism. Neither have I in twenty-three years of ministry.
2. He discerned that the people he met were depressed and in some instances, presumably, oppressed by the Evil One.
3. He delivered them from their troubles in a spirit of gentleness and compassion, by administering the sacraments of reconciliation and the Eucharist. They have great power to
   – absolve sin;
   – to heal the memory and hurting emotions;

    – to deliver from evil influences, and

    – to strengthen the person for the future.

4. He told them that they were healed, with such expectant faith that he evoked a similar conviction in those who had come to him for help.

5. Everyone went away comforted and healed.

In my experience, this is a good way of dealing with spiritual oppression. The person suffering in this way can go to a wise, compassionate and discerning priest or lay person for prayer. Added to that, he or she can have recourse to the sacraments of reconciliation, Eucharist, and anointing, with a firm conviction that they can both deliver and protect a person from the influence of the Evil One.

For example, a few years ago a teenage girl I met when I was working in a hospital, told me that she was under the influence of an evil spirit. Mary said that it had all started when she began reading people's palms and found that she could apparently tell them about their past and future. Sometime later she was disturbed by apparitions of her dead grandmother. My instinctive reaction was one of belief. But it was quickly followed by a more rational type of incredulity. It was hard to believe that such a young girl could be oppressed by an evil spirit. I presumed that there was some psychological or physical explanation for her state of mind. I discussed her case with a neurologist, a psychiatrist, a number of priests, two experienced exorcists, and a theologian who was familiar with this kind of problem. After a two-month assessment process a consensus emerged. The facts were pointing towards the probability of spiritual oppression. Having prepared for some time by prayer and fasting, I heard Mary's confession, anointed her while asking God to deliver her from evil, and to fill and protect her with his Holy Spirit. Shortly after her release from hospital, she wrote to thank me for my prayers. Mary said that the oppressing sense of evil had left her, and that her occult powers had been replaced by an inward sense of peace.

Conclusion

While most mental and emotional problems can be explained in psychological terms, there are some cases which can only be understood in terms of demonic influence. So, if psychiatrists operate out of a purely secular world-view, they will take little or no account of this dimension. Consequently, it is not surprising that their treatments can fail to achieve satisfactory results. ECT and tranquilizers have no power to deliver a person from oppression by an evil spirit! Three things are needed. Firstly, a world-view that has a spiritual dimension. Secondly, an ability to discern whether personality problems may be partly due to the influence of an evil spirit. Thirdly, a conviction that if we have reason to pray for deliverance, then God, in his love, will hear our prayer.

TACTICS OF THE EVIL ONE

Ignatius of Loyola was born into a Basque family in Northern Spain. As a member of the nobility he was rich, preoccupied with personal and familial glory, and like his father and brothers, devoted to worldly pleasures. When he reached adulthood he became a soldier and in 1521 he sustained a very bad leg wound during a siege. Afterwards, during an extended convalescence, he underwent a religious conversion. He decided to become a soldier of Christ in the battle against evil. A year later, following a number of mystical experiences at Manresa, he wrote his *Spiritual Exercises*.

In a section of his religious classic, which is full of medieval imagery, Ignatius says that there are two kingdoms on earth, the Kingdom of God, and the kingdom of Satan. Whether they know it or not, everyone owes allegiance to one or the other. Four centuries later, Bob Dylan echoed the same sentiment in one of his songs. There is 'no neutral ground', he says in the lyrics, 'You have got to serve someone. It may be the Devil, or it may be the Lord, but you have got to serve someone.' In his Exercises, Ignatius goes on to ask the all-important question: how does the evil spirit lead people away from God into his service? His answer is at once perceptive and relevant. The Devil achieves his purposes in subtle and indirect ways, by successively prompting people to desire fortune, fame and freedom from objective ethical restraints.

The desire for riches
The Devil begins to influence people in an innocuous way, by inspiring them to desire riches. As scripture warns us, 'The love of money is a root of all kinds of evil, and in their eagerness to be rich some have wandered away from the faith' (1 Tm 6:10). Needless to say, this desire refers principally to money and material things. But it can also refer to any created thing which

promises fulfilment without transcendence, e.g. knowledge, education, qualifications, relationships, human development, artistic and sporting pursuits etc. Although these things are obviously good in themselves, people may unwittingly identify with one or more of them as having absolute value.[1] Then, there is a danger that these things will become, albeit at an unconscious level, latter-day golden calves, idols to be worshipped as substitutes for God.

The desire for reputation

The second stage of this subversive dynamic is reached when, possessing the things they desired, people find themselves seeking status, honour and a good reputation. Again, there isn't anything necessarily wrong with these desires unless they become absolutely important. At an unconscious level, victims of these possibly idolatrous needs may be obsessed, on the one hand, by a desire for the approval and esteem of others, and, on the other, by a deep-seated fear of forfeiting them. Not surprisingly, they become susceptible to jealousy, envy, resentment and the like. Worldly desires can also be betrayed by their compulsive and addictive nature.

Speaking of compulsiveness, Henri Nouwen has observed[2] that 'obsessive' is the best adjective for the worldly, false self. It needs ongoing and increased recognition, affirmation and approval. Who am I? I am the one who is liked, praised, admired, accepted....What matters is how I am perceived by the world. If being busy is a good thing, I must be busy. If having money is a sign of real freedom, then I must get more money. If knowing people proves my importance, I will have to make as many contacts as possible. If being successful will impress others, then I'd better excel in whatever I do. The compulsive nature of these desires also manifests itself in a pathological fear of losing face.

Commenting on the related issue of addictive desires, psychiatrist Gerald May has pointed out that 'addiction is a state of compulsion, obsession, or preoccupation that enslaves a person's will and desire. Addiction sidetracks and eclipses the energy of our deepest, truest desire for love and goodness.'[3] In our culture, where the pursuit of worldly security and honours has often been substituted for conscious relationship with God, it is not surprising that the incidence of all forms of addiction has increased. Some people become hooked on substances like alcohol, tranquilizers, sleeping pills and hard drugs. Others become workaholics, while approximately one in twelve of the population develops a sexual addiction.

The desire for independence

The third and final phase of this insidious process leads to a subtle perversion of values. Once a person, group or nation is rich and well-thought-of, unacknowledged pride motivates an overriding of the dictates of the moral law in order to suit themselves. They rationalise their reasons for doing so, while referring perhaps to the rights of conscience. For example, adulterers try to validate their infidelities in the name of true love. Extreme nationalists try to justify their resentments and violent actions in the name of justice. Unscrupulous business people try to explain away their shady practices in the name of economic expediency. Nation states try to rationalise their Machiavellian policies in the name of political idealism. Speaking from an objective point of view, however, St John reminds us of the chilling implications: 'Everyone who does wrong is a child of the Devil' (1 Jn 3:8).

Moral relativism

It seems that despite their good points, liberal democracies tend to reinforce the moral relativism just mentioned. As a result, they can make people more vulnerable to the illusions, false inspirations and temptations of the Evil One. Even when they are acting in conscious good faith, people can end up doing things that are intrinsically evil from an objective standpoint.

In his recent book, *Understanding the Present*,[4] Brian Appleyard has shown, in a convincing way, why this can be so. He indicates how, imitating the neutrality of science, contemporary governments avoid committing themselves to any specific values and beliefs. Instead they try to create frameworks of law which are designed to accommodate the competing and often contradictory values and beliefs of different social groups. So the prevailing cultural ethos is pluralistic and relativistic. For secular humanists, and many others, knowledge and, therefore, all beliefs and values, are provisional. Because no objective realm of unchanging meaning can be invoked, all values are necessarily subjective. Because he acknowledged this to be the case, John L. McKenzie made the striking, if questionable assertion in *The Civilisation of Christianity* that there is a deadly and irreconcilable opposition between civilisation and Christianity and that, sooner or later, one of them must succumb to the other.

There is a disturbing residue of truth, however, in what McKenzie says. As Cardinal Hume has written, 'For some, morality has become, in our individualistic age, a matter of private opinions and choices, in which there are no longer any objective standards for judging right and wrong.'[5] Because religious people live within secular society, they are constantly tempted to abandon the demanding teachings of revealed morality, in favour of a watered down, à la carte approach to decision making. As St Paul warns, 'God gave them up to a debased mind and to things that should not be done' (Rm 1:28). Surely this subjectivism and relativism are being exploited by the Evil One for his malevolent purposes.

Many religious people believe that, as a result of divine revelation and rational reflection, we can become aware of the commandments of God and the natural law. They are universal and apply to all without exception. In a recent letter, *Veritatis Splendor*, addressed to the bishops of the Roman Catholic Church, Pope John Paul II stated that there are some actions which are always seriously wrong. For example, anything which is hostile to human life or the integrity and dignity of the human person such as abortion, child sexual abuse, genocide, and the exploitation of labour, is intrinsically evil. As a result, intentions, circumstances and consequences can never make them right.

Of course, not everyone, would agree with this point of view, not even within the Catholic Church. But what if John Paul is correct? If he is, then the subjective and conscientious beliefs of secular society will not change the objective state of things. While people may not be doing evil in their own eyes, they may well be doing evil in the sight of God. If so, the results will be inevitable. While God in his mercy will excuse the ignorance and blindness of people who do wrong actions in good faith, such wrongdoing will tend, nevertheless, to cause alienation both within and between people. It will also bring about the affliction and breakdown of society. That has already happened twice in this century, with horrendous results. I was deeply moved by these poignant and prophetic words of John Paul II in his encyclical *Redemptor Hominis*: 'If any of our contemporaries,' he writes, 'do not share the faith and hope which lead me, as servant of Christ and steward of the mysteries of God, to implore God's mercy for humanity in this hour of history, let them at least try to understand the reason for my concern. It is dictated by love for people, for all that is human and which, according to the intuitions of many of our contemporaries, *is threatened by an immense* danger' (italics mine) (nn. 15-17).

Perhaps Bernard Lonergan was one of the contemporaries that the Pope had in mind. He has described, in a cogent and disturbing way, how whole societies can experience decline as a result of such things as selfishness, subjectivism and a lack of transcendental awareness. When values and beliefs get 'corrupted,' to use Lonergan's word, they are disseminated by the mass media, the education system and the prevailing philosophies of the time. "A civilisation in decline," he concludes, "digs its own grave with relentless consistency. It cannot be argued out of its destructive way."[6]

In the coming years it is possible that, as a result of growing irrationality and moral blindness, we may have to endure a time of economic and political disruption. After all, we have experienced at least two such upheavals in the twentieth century. No matter how painful the dislocation of society may be, it could lead many people to reject questionable philosophical and economic beliefs, just as it has already done in the former Soviet Union. If that time comes, perhaps large numbers of disillusioned people will finally take heed of these prophetic words: 'Seek the Lord while he may be found, call upon him while he is near; let the wicked forsake their way' (Is 55:6).

Deliver us from evil

How do people and nations escape the devastating influence of evil? This is a huge question. But here are a few brief suggestions.

Firstly, we need to recover an objective sense of right and wrong, especially the vital importance of genuine love in all ethical decision-making. As Jesus said, 'In everything, do to others as you would have them do to you; for this is the law and the prophets' (Mt 7:12).

Secondly, we need to reverse the worldly tendencies described by Ignatius of Loyola. Instead of focusing exclusively on human fulfilment, we need to reach beyond ourselves, by growing in conscious relationship with the mystery of God. Instead of wanting worldly glory, we need to be humble and modest, acknowledging that all the good things we possess are the gift of God. Instead of wanting to do our own wilful thing, we need to discover what the loving Spirit of God is prompting us to do.

Thirdly, we need to discern what spirit is moving us when we are making decisions. Is it our human spirit, the Holy Spirit, or the Evil Spirit? Put briefly, it can be said that only those inspirations that come from God are inwardly associated with a sense of ongoing peace and joy. The others lead, sooner or later, to sadness, agitation and restlessness of spirit. (For more on this subject, see chapter 13.)

Finally, when we are tempted to do what we know to be wrong, we need to nestle, rather than wrestle. It is a matter of nestling in God by faith, instead of wrestling alone with temptation. As St Paul says, 'Put on the whole armour of God that you may be able to stand against the wiles of the devil.' (Ep 6:11). As a later chapter indicates, we will find that 'God is faithful, and he will not let us be tested beyond our strength, but with the testing he will also provide the way out so that we may be able to endure it' (1 Co 10:13).

8

THE AWARENESS OF SIN

Some time ago, psychologist Karl Menninger wrote a book with the thought-provoking title, *Whatever Happened to Sin?* Recently, during a period when I was conducting parish missions around Ireland, I often asked myself the same question. As I searched for an answer, I became increasingly aware of two interrelated things.

Firstly, like many non-church-goers, some church-goers haven't yet been fully evangelised. In spite of the fact that they receive the sacraments, they often fail to mature as followers of Christ. I think that this is mainly due to the fact that they have never experienced a spiritual awakening. Only such a breakthrough would enable them to develop a deep personal relationship with Jesus. This can only occur when adults have a religious experience, an inner assurance, which inaugurates a new and decisive awareness of 'the length and breadth, the height and depth, of the love of Christ which surpasses understanding' (Ep 3:18). This consciousness can fill them with a new and illuminating sense, both of God and of themselves.

Secondly, those who have failed to become consciously aware of the merciful love of God in this way, tend to have an unrealistic attitude to sin. On the one hand, those with a subjectivist view of morality seem to be blissfully ignorant of most of their wrongdoings and omissions, while, on the other hand, those with a legalistic view of morality, are so painfully aware of both, that they become scrupulous and weighed down with a neurotic sense of guilt. In this chapter we will take a brief look at each of these distorted attitudes.

Pseudo-innocence

Here is a typical scene that I have seen re-enacted time and time again. A young man, dressed in jeans and leather jacket, comes into the confessional. Immediately he says in a bright and breezy way, 'Hi, Father, how's it going.' Having told him that things are going okay for me, I make the sign of the cross, say a prayer for guidance, and begin. 'How long is it since your last confession?' 'I'm not sure, Father,' he replies. 'It's a few years anyway, probably four or five.' 'And do you think that during those years you did anything, or for that matter, failed to do anything, that you feel particularly sorry about just now?' 'No, not really, Father, things have been going well for me.' 'I'm glad to hear that,' I respond, while trying to hide my incredulity and growing irritation. 'Have you ever failed to show love to the people you know, ever said an insensitive word, reacted in a negative way because of resentment, jealousy, or envy?' 'No, Father, I get on well with everyone... But I suppose that I may have told the odd lie, or used bad language sometimes.' By and large, I don't pursue the matter any further. I'm glad the person has come to receive the sacrament of reconciliation. His very presence is a sign of good will. Knowing God has forgiven him, I give him absolution. However, I suspect that having confessed, like so many others, in a superficial way, the young man will only feel superficially forgiven.

Why is it that so many people are victims of what Rollo May has aptly referred to as pseudo-innocence? It seems to me that a realistic awareness of sin presupposes a number of things. Firstly, from a subjective point of view, people need to have a certain degree of self-awareness. Although most people are well-educated and knowledgeable, they can be surprisingly out of touch, not only with with their deeper feelings, attitudes and motives, but also with the quiet murmurings of their consciences. Perhaps this is one of the principal effects of living in an overly extroverted, materialistic culture. Pope Paul VI once said that modern men and women are 'totally extroverted, they are under the spell of exterior life, so charming, fascinating and corrupting with its delusions of false happiness.'[1] On another occasion he said, 'Today our psychology is turned outward too much. The exterior scene is so absorbing that our attention is mainly directed outside; we are nearly always absent from our personal abode....We cannot silence the hubbub inside, due to outside interests, images and passions.'[2] A second cause of spiritual blindness, as we have already noted, is that people need to have a personal relationship with Christ, because it is only in the light of his love that sin, as a failure to love, is truly revealed.

Another reason for pseudo-innocence, is that the words 'sin' and 'sinfulness' do not accurately describe the inner experience of many Christians. They probably say too little when they refer to external faults rather than to internal attitudes. They say too much because people tend to associate them with vague feelings of unworthiness. These feelings often include a sense of being unlovable and worthless, attitudes that were probably formed in childhood before they ever committed any faults. Not surprisingly, the self-esteem of people like this is easily threatened by talk about sin and sinfulness. Consequently, their feelings of inferiority and insecurity are inclined to paralyse them, thereby preventing them from acknowledging their wrongdoings. I think that there are two interwoven reasons for this tendency.

Negative images of God and denial

To begin with, I suspect that many people have positive concepts of God, e.g. as tender-hearted and compassionate; while at an unconscious level they have negative images of God, e.g. as demanding and vindictive. In all likelihood they formed such images in childhood as a result of intimidating experiences of authority. Then, in a culture where the emphasis is on conscience and personal rights rather than on objective standards and duties, people with negative images of God, can end up by adopting the unthreatening requirements of an undemanding morality, where the focus is on self-fulfilment rather than self-transcendence. Troubling feelings of guilt are wrongly suppressed as being unhealthy and neurotic. Instead, there is a lot of talk about unconditional acceptance and understanding. It is true that in Luke 6:36-39, Jesus told us not to judge or condemn ourselves or other people. But in the name of truth and honesty, it is necessary to judge and condemn bad actions and omissions. As Augustine said in *The City of God*, some people condemn the sinner because they condemn the sin, others love the sin because they love the sinner, but Christians should condemn the sin while loving the sinner.[3]

It is often said that many modern Christians have lost a sense of sin. I don't think that such an opinion is entirely true. After all, many people are painfully aware, not so much of particular sins, as of a generalised sense of unworthiness and of being alienated from the God whom they long to know and love. But they do find it hard to admit responsibility for particular sinful acts and omissions which may have contributed to this state of affairs. Their wrongdoings are excused on the basis of their genes, upbringing, temperament, past hurts, environmental influences etc. Like Adam in the Garden of Eden, they blame someone or something else, saying, 'It's not my fault....such and such made me do it!' As we shall see in the next chapter, such Christians need a foundational experience of the loving mercy of God, one that will reveal their sinfulness within an atmosphere of psychological and spiritual safety.

Scrupulosity and neurotic guilt

When hearing confessions, one meets adults who are all too aware of sin and guilt. In fact they are preoccupied with both. For example, an old woman comes into the box. She is wearing a heavy tweed overcoat, and is donning a hat with a feather in it. You can almost hear her joints creaking, as she slowly kneels with difficulty. Immediately she begins, 'Bless me father, I have sinned, it is thirteen days since my last confession, I'd like to make a general confession.' I say, 'of course', and she begins to talk in a troubled voice about the sins of her youth. Clearly, they were against the sixth commandment. She tries as best she can to hint at the nature of her wrongdoings. However, she finds it hard to do so because she feels so embarrassed and ashamed. Although I try to encourage her, by saying that she needn't go into all the details, she doesn't seem to hear, and tries again to tell her story. Her attention is upon the way in which she makes her confession, rather than on the mercy and love of God. She is terrified that if she doesn't get it right, if she doesn't dot all her 'i's and cross all her 't's God will reject her. Even when I'm assuring her that all her sins are forgiven and forgotten, the ones she can remember, the ones she finds hard to mention, the ones she has forgotten, and the ones she isn't even aware of, she interrupts and says, 'Oh, Father, there is something else that I forgot to mention!' Finally, I give her absolution. But I suspect that although she may feel relieved, she won't feel that she is forgiven. In the future she will go to another priest, and tell him exactly the same list of sins, especially the ones of her youth. Why is it that people become as scrupulous as this? I think that Freud has helped us to understand the reason. Instead of having a healthy and realistic sense of guilt, moralistic people suffer from a neurotic, superego guilt.

Freud's theory of personality is based on a conflict between what he called the id, the ego and the superego. The id is the seat of instinctual drives which are guided by the pleasure principle, e.g. a need for sexual satisfaction. The id is amoral, largely unconscious and partly revealed in dreams, e.g. making love to a family member. The ego embraces the person's conscious self-awareness as it relates in a realistic way to the outer world of people and events and the inner reality of thoughts, memories, feelings etc. The ego is oriented toward relationships, values and beliefs which are accepted as a result of personal conviction. The superego represents the internalised values and attitudes of significant others, such as parents, carers, teachers and clergy. It manifests itself in the form of authoritative conscience and a strong sense of duty. In its healthy form it helps to mediate the traditional values of Church, society and family. In its unhealthy form it is moralistic and overbearing, threatening to withdraw love and approval from the personality if it fails to live up to its personal demands and ideals.

How the unhealthy superego develops

How does an unhealthy superego develop?[4] Freud argued that when a baby is very small, it is helpless and totally dependent on its parents (or parental substitutes) for clothes, food and shelter. It is motivated and energised by a bundle of undisciplined and selfish needs and desires. So, in an effort to socialise the child, its parents have to discipline it. They may give the impression in verbal and non-verbal ways that they will have a greater love for their child if it behaves; if it doesn't urinate on the carpet; if it doesn't put jam on the wallpaper; if it doesn't cry too much, etc.

Although the child desires to do its own thing, it desires the apparently conditional love of its parents even more. So it learns to conform to their expectations in order to retain their affection and acceptance. As the child develops, it begins to internalise the values and attitudes of its parents, in the form of conscience. This is what Freud referred to as the Superego. Its demands often become synonymous with the demands of God. As a result, if either the growing child or, later, the mature adult, indulges in any forbidden instinctual behaviour, e.g. of a sexual kind, the unhealthy superego may say, 'Because you did a bad thing, you are a bad person, you can no longer love or accept yourself, and the same is true of God, he doesn't love or accept you either.'

Effects of an unhealthy superego

The unhealthy superego is conformist and perfectionist in its outlook, is motivated by external authority, i.e. the expectations of others, and expresses itself in the language of obligation, e.g. 'I must, I ought, I have to, I should do such and such.' As a result of this hardening of the 'oughteries,' the personality hasn't much inner authority. It rarely expresses itself in the language of conviction, e.g. 'I need, I desire, I believe, I want such and such.' People with unhealthy superegos tend to be critical, judgemental and condemnatory in their thoughts and words. They treat others as badly as they already treat themselves. They are inclined to project their guilt on to others by seeing the splinter in their neighbour's eye while failing to acknowledge the plank in their own.

Whenever people with unhealthy superegos fail to live up to their idealistic standards, they not only feel that they are bad and unlovable, they can also suffer feelings of remorse, alienation, isolation, anxiety and mild depression. As I mention later in the book, these negative emotions can arouse instinctual desires, often of a sexual kind, as a way of revitalising their personalities. One psychologist has suggested[5] that rather than being rooted in lustful desires, up to eighty-five per cent of our sexual fantasies and deeds are rooted in such negative inward states. However, if for largely unconscious reasons, the person happens to offend against the dictates of conscience, he or she experiences even greater anxiety, and a vicious circle is completed.

Instead of seeing sin in terms of relationship, as a failure to respond to the unconditional love of God, people with superego problems tend to see it in terms of impersonal moral principles, as a failure to keep the law. They are sorry for their sins, not because they withdrew their love from God, but because they are afraid that God has withdrawn what they feel is his conditional love from them. Like the old woman, they go to confession in order to placate the God of harsh justice and to win back his love and approval. They put their faith in the *way* in which they confess their sins, e.g. mentioning their number and kind, rather than in the loving mercy of God. So, not surprisingly, many of them tend to be scrupulous. In biblical terms, instead of living by faith, they continue to live by law.

More often than not, when they receive absolution they experience relief rather than genuine peace. They get back to square one, but because there is no real growth in their relationship with God, there is no real opportunity for change in their personalities. They may have the desire to do better in the future, but they don't have the ability to do so. As a result, despite their purpose of amendment, they will tend to repeat the same sins and confessions, time and time again.

How to overcome an unhealthy superego

1. Avoid asking what you ought to do. In the light of your relationship with the Lord and with other people ask yourself what it is that you would want to do.

2. In prayer, focus on the unconditional love of God.

3. Try to see moral values in terms of conscious relationship with God, rather than in terms of impersonal laws.

4. If you are going to confession, ask the God who searches every heart, to search yours to help you to know your sin, i.e. the areas in your life where you failed to receive and to respond to the unconditional love of God.

5. Ask the Lord for the grace of perfect contrition, i.e. feeling sorry for your sins, not because you have a morbid and mistaken fear that God has withdrawn his supposedly conditional love from you, but because you have selfishly withdrawn your love from the Lord.

6. Meditate upon one or more of the following texts:
   - Luke 15:11-32 – the story of the prodigal son.
     - The younger, son who indulges his desires without restraint, represents the amoral and hedonistic urges of the id.
     - The father, who is compassionate, accepting, understanding and generous, represents the Christian ego which is aware of the merciful love of God.
     - The elder brother, who is dutiful, judgemental and harsh, represents the unhealthy superego.
   - Luke 7:35-50 – the story of the woman who washed the feet of Jesus.
     - Mary, the prostitute, who indulged the desires of the flesh represents the id.
     - Jesus, in his love, understanding and disregard of public opinion, represents the Christian ego.
     - Simon, the Pharisee, who is impersonal, critical and moralistic, represents the unhealthy superego.
   - Luke 18:9-15 – the Pharisee and the tax collector.
     - The tax collector, who is dishonest and disloyal, symbolises the id.
     - Jesus, who is discerning and compassionate, is like the Christian ego.
     - The pharisee, who is proud, dutiful, judgemental and self-righteous, represents the unhealthy superego.

Conclusion

I suspect that although people who suffer from pseudo-innocence and scrupulosity seem to be very different, they are in fact very alike. They are united by their shared fear of God. In the case of the former it is conscious, in the case of latter it is unconscious. But for both, their fear and their guilt lead to the civil war of the heart, the disastrous inner split between Jung's acceptable and the unacceptable self. They will not be able to accept themselves until they can acknowledge their sins in the light of God's love, and know that instead of being condemned, they are being declared not guilty and acquitted by the reconciling grace of God. As long as people live under the shadow of real, but unacknowledged guilt, they will not be able to accept themselves, to be themselves, or to forget themselves in outgoing love for others. Until they do, all the well-intentioned efforts of friends, counsellors and spiritual directors, to reassure them, will be in vain. They will continue to hate themselves and to suffer the inevitable consequences of self-hatred. As we shall see in the next chapter, the moment they accept their sinfulness and guilt, the possibility of radical Christian transformation opens up. As it does, such people, through the action of justifying grace, pass from a deep and pervasive self-rejection to a new-found freedom, self-respect and peace.

9

VICTORY OVER SIN

Recently, I was interested to see that after spending a lifetime writing about people and events, historian and philosopher Will Durant came to an emphatic conclusion. At the venerable age of ninety-two, he distilled more than two thousand years of history into three simple words: 'Love one another'. 'My final lesson of history,' he wrote, 'is the same as that of Jesus. You may think it is a lot of bunkum, but just try it. Love is the most practical thing in the world.'

In the light of love

During the summer of 1993, I had an illuminating experience during my annual retreat. On a number of occasions I prayed, in the words of St Paul, that I would have power to comprehend... the breadth and length and height and depth...of the love of Christ' (Ep 3:18). Then, one evening, my prayer was answered as I knelt before the blessed sacrament. Suddenly, in my mind's eye I saw Jesus standing in front of the altar. He was young and attractive looking. He wore a simple one piece garment and red and white light was shining downward from his hands. When he briefly raised his palms there was a momentary flash of light from each. Then he lowered them a bit, until I found myself standing in the gentle glow of the converging beams.

Inwardly I knew myself to be standing in the light of God's mercy and love. I was reminded of the text which says, 'Rays came forth from his hands where his power lies hidden' (Hab 3:4). My spirit seemed to be illumined. The words, 'We have known and believe the love God has for us' (1 Jn 4:16), encapsulated my new-found awareness and revealed a number of spiritual truths to me.

Human and divine love

To begin with, I had a deepened appreciation of the *agape* nature of God's love, which is unconditional and unrestricted.

Over the years I have noticed there are two forms of human love, one needy, the other responsive. The first says, 'I love you because I need you...need you to provide me with financial security...social status...emotional support...sexual satisfaction etc.

Does God love us because he needs us? I don't think so. There is nothing we can offer him that he hasn't already given to us. We could paraphrase the fourth weekday Preface of the Mass to read, 'God has no need of anything we can offer him, our desire to give good things is itself his gift. Our offerings add nothing to his greatness, but help us to grow in his grace, through Jesus Christ our Lord.'

The second form of human love says, 'I need you because I love you. Having perceived your inner worth and value I find myself responding to your goodness by spontaneously approving of you, and wanting what is best for you.'

Well then, does God love us because he is responding to our inner worth and value? Again I don't think so. Although he is delighted to see our inner merit, his love doesn't depend on it. God's love is freely given with no strings attached. It is the expression of *his* nature, rather than a response to ours. The truth is, God is incapable of not loving us. As scripture assures us, he has no favourites (cf. Acts 10:34). As a result, presumably, he gratuitously loves you and me just as much as he loves Mother Teresa of Calcutta, or the worst criminal in prison. This realisation has important and liberating effects.

Divine love and self-awareness

Firstly, instead of discovering my identity by means of introspection and emotional self-awareness, what is innermost within me can only be truly revealed in the light of God's mercy and love. The fourteenth-century English mystic, Dame Julian of Norwich, was aware of this. She would have agreed with the contention that we are so wounded and blinded by feelings of guilt and worthlessness that we cannot know ourselves rightly apart from the affirming and recreative experience of God's loving mercy. She wrote in her *Showings*: 'I saw most surely that it is quicker for us and easier to come to the knowledge of God than it is to know our own soul. For our soul is so deeply grounded in God and so endlessly

treasured that we cannot come to knowledge of it until we first
have knowledge of God, who is the Creator to whom it is
united....God is closer to us than our own soul, for he is the foun-
dation on which our soul stands....For our soul sits in God in true
rest, and our soul stands in God in sure strength, and our soul is
naturally rooted in God in endless love. And therefore if we want
to have knowledge of our soul, and communion and discourse
with it, we must seek it in our Lord God in whom it is enclosed.'[1]
In our own century Thomas Merton echoed this assertion when
he said in a conference on prayer, 'Who am I? My deepest realisation of who I am is – I am one loved by Christ.... The depths of
my identity is in the centre of my being where I am known by
God.'[2] Pope John Paul says much the same in paragraph 8 of
Veritatis Splendor. 'The man who wishes to understand himself
thoroughly,' he states, 'must draw near to Christ. He must, so to
speak, enter him with all his self; he must "appropriate" and
assimilate the whole of the reality of the Incarnation and
Redemption in *order to find himself.* If this profound process takes
place within him, he then bears the fruit not only of adoration
but also of *deeper wonder at himself* (italics mine).

Sin is revealed in the light of divine love

In the second place, as I come to know myself in the light of
God's love, the true nature of my sinfulness is revealed. Instead
of being aware of what was sinful in my own eyes, as heretofore,
I become aware of what is sinful in the eyes of God. Just as the
light on a summer's day reveals the dust on window-sills and
table-tops, so the light of God's love reveals the lack of love in
my life. As scripture rightly says, the Lord 'gradually corrects
those who offend; by admonishing and reminding them of how
they have sinned' (Ws 12:2). I realise that all too often I am
motivated by selfishness, or merely human love, of a needy or
responsive kind. Not only that, in the radiance of divine love I
become aware that my shortcomings have not only grieved the
Holy Spirit, they have also led me – unwittingly perhaps – to be
duped by the illusions and false inspirations of the Evil One. As
St John reminds us, 'Whoever lives sinfully belongs to the Devil,
since the Devil has been a sinner from the beginning....We are

well aware that no one who is a child of God sins, because he who was born from God protects him, and the Evil One has no hold over him' (1 Jn 3:8; 5:18). This newfound awareness prompts an inner detestation of sin as something alien to the love of God, and to one's true identity in Christ. Like the Prodigal Son, who finally came to his senses, I experienced a God-prompted desire to give up my former way of living and to draw closer to God.

Power to change

When, in the past, my sins were revealed in the light of the law, I may have had the desire to change but didn't often have the power to do so, because impersonal rules and regulations didn't provide such power. As Kathryn Kuhlman once wryly observed, 'That is just the difficulty in many partly changed lives. The joy of sinning is gone. But the fact of sinning is not. It is still there...You have just enough religion to make you miserable in your sinning, but not enough to make you masterful through your Saviour.'[3] But when God reveals my sin in the light of his love, I not only have a desire to change, I also have the Spirit-given power to do so. As Kathryn Kuhlman reminds us, 'there is a power that is available whereby any man or woman can overcome their weakness... You may be aware of your weakness, but you are more conscious of the mighty power that is sustaining you. 'I can do all things through him who strengthens me' (Ph 4:13).'[4]

Whereas the power of sin is rooted in my old nature, the power to live a sinless life is rooted in my new nature in Christ. As St Paul says in Romans 6:4, 'Our former self was crucified with him, so that the self which belonged to sin should be destroyed and we should be set free from slavery to sin.' It is significant that he says that 'our former self was crucified'. The change has already been effected. It has already been accomplished in principle. That is why I can be confident that it can also be accomplished in fact. It will be, if I live by faith in the power of my new identity in Christ, the sinless One. In Romans 6:2, St Paul goes so far as to say, 'We have died to sin.' It is not that we *will* die, or *are* dying, but that we have *already* died to sin. If I am still aware of the urgings, and the apparent power of my old nature, it is rather like the ghost pains experienced by a person who has had a limb amputated. It is a salutary reminder of something that used to be there, but is no longer so.

In this connection I was both amused and helped by a story told by the late David Watson in his book *God's Freedom Fighters.*[5] There was once this man who was convinced he was dead. His friends tried in vain to show him that he was really alive. Eventually they brought him to a psychiatrist who told him that dead men don't bleed. Then, to prove his point, he showed his patient many textbooks which illustrated the point in graphic terms. After some time the man said, 'I accept your point, doctor, dead men don't bleed.' As soon as he said this, the psychiatrist grabbed a paper-knife and struck the man on his arm. Immediately, drops of blood appeared. When he saw this, the deluded man looked shocked and exclaimed, 'Well, well, dead men bleed, after all!' Here was a person who felt he was dead. Objective facts made no impression on him at all. It can be the same with me as far as sin is concerned. I may feel that my old, sinful nature is all-powerful, while ignoring the fact that in Christ I am already dead to sin. As long as I affirm my new identity in Christ, and the power I have in him, sin will wither. Besides tackling specific faults in my life, I will need to avoid predictable occasions of sin as best I can. I will also need to be confident that, although I will be tempted in the future, I will have the power to resist as long as I rely solely on the grace of God. For more on this, see the next chapter. As St Paul said, 'God is faithful, he will not let you be tempted beyond what you can bear. But when you are tempted he will provide a way out so that you can stand up under it' (1 Co 10:3).

The golden rule of love
As the light of God's Spirit transforms my life it will urge me to publish and make known the love that is innermost within my heart, by loving others as Christ has loved me. I can do this by observing the golden rule which states, 'Always treat others the way you would like them to treat you; that is the meaning of the law and the prophets' (Mt 7:12). To do this, I need to go

beyond the limitations of need and responsive love, 'to love as Jesus loved'. I can do this by struggling, with the help of God, to offer unconditional empathy and approval to other people, especially those who are difficult and unattractive from a human point of view. As Vincent de Paul once said about this kind of love, 'it enables hearts to enter into each other and feel what the other feels. It is far removed from the sort of people who have no feeling for the pain of those who suffer or for the plight of the poor.'[6]

If I learn to love people in a compassionate, non-judgmental way, they may begin to see themselves as God sees them. As their innermost dignity is published and made known in the light of creative Christian love, they may begin to accept themselves, to be themselves, and to forget themselves in outgoing love of others. As St John of the Cross once observed, where there is no love, put love, and you will receive love. By loving I prepare myself for another intimate encounter with the Lord, the one that will occur at the moment of my death.

Examined in love

Recently I was very impressed by something that Dr Raymond Moody said in a published interview.[7] He is the author of the well-known book, *Life after Life*, and was commenting on the near-death experiences of patients who had been resuscitated after their clinical deaths had occurred. I have presumed to paraphrase his words. 'They become aware of a tunnel, or passageway. They go into this passageway and come out into a warm and brilliant light. In this light they see relatives and friends who have already died. At this point Christian people say that they are met by Christ. In a wordless way he asks, "What have you done with your life? Have you learned to love?" This question triggers a profoundly intimate experience. All that was innermost in their experience is published and made known. They undergo an exhaustive review of all the main events of their lives. They are displayed around them in a detailed, three-dimensional way.

'The patients often report that during this life review they evaluate the events of their lives not from the perspective they had when they went through them, but rather from a third-person perspective. In other words, they stand inside the skin of anyone they have been unkind to and experience his or her negative emotions. On the other hand, if they see an action where they were loving to someone, they can feel the warmth and good feelings that had been evoked in that person. Interestingly, the review has nothing to do with the earthly success, financial well-being, and power that preoccupies so many of us.' It is worth noting that every one of the people who confided in Moody told him that they were faced with two questions. Firstly, had they learned to love? And, secondly, had they put this love into practice in their lives?

The general judgement

The coming of Christ at the time of our death is a preparation for his final coming at the end of history. Then he will judge the living and the dead. It will be a day of supreme intimacy, when everything hidden will be published and made known in the presence of everyone who has ever lived. Using the criterion of love alone, God will separate the sheep from the goats. The goats, i.e. those who failed to show love, will be cast into eternal darkness. Devoid of love they will be forever alienated from God and therefore from their true selves and from others. The sheep, on the other hand, i.e. those who tried to express unconditional love in their lives, will enter light inaccessible. Then, the Holy Spirit who searches the hidden depths of God will illumine and make known what is innermost in his divine nature. In the light of that definitive revelation, those who have been saved will know themselves and one another in the ecstatic joy of unending Love.

10

FREEDOM FROM ADDICTION

The origin of English words can be fascinating and revealing. The word 'addiction' is a case in point. It comes from the Latin *ad,* meaning 'to', and *dicere,* which literally means to 'say' or 'pronounce'. Apparently it can be traced back to the Roman courts, where a judge could pronounce that a person was bound over into the power and control of someone else who would be his lord and master. So we suffer from an addiction when we lose our inner freedom by falling under the power and control of some created thing. In his book *Addiction and Grace,* Christian psychiatrist Gerald May defines an addiction as 'any compulsive, habitual behaviour that limits the freedom of human desire. It is caused by attachment, or nailing, of desire to specific objects.'[1]

Gerald May suggests[2] that there are two main kinds of addiction, namely process addictions such as angry perfectionism, compulsive fear, an overweening need for approval etc.; and substance addictions, such as being hooked on alcohol, valium, nicotine, sleeping pills, hard drugs etc. He also suggests that addictions can be looked at from two perspectives. Firstly, there are attraction addictions, i.e. ones in which we find something pleasurable. There are hundreds of them such as eating, watching TV, smoking etc. Secondly, there are aversion addictions, i.e. ones where we find something repulsive. Again, there are hundreds of them, such as fear of failure, aversion to pain etc. While many of us think that only certain groups of people such as alcoholics and drug abusers are addicted, the fact is that all of us suffer from addictions. So, the question is not, 'Do you have an addiction?' but, rather, 'What addictions do you suffer from?' That said, it is true, of course, that some addictions, such as alcoholism and gambling, are more destructive than others, such as watching TV or gardening. Nevertheless, despite their apparent differences, they are similar from a psychological and spiritual point of view.

Civil war of the heart

Why do people develop addictions? Mother Teresa says it is because many in our society suffer from a famine of genuine love. Carl Jung would have endorsed this point of view. In chapter 3 we saw how he believed that all our psychological and moral problems can be traced back to the civil war of the heart, the split between the acceptable and the unacceptable self. He wrote: 'Neurosis is a splitting of personality... it is an inner cleavage – the state of being at war with oneself. Everything that accentuates this cleavage makes the patient worse, and everything that mitigates it tends to heal him.'[3] Jung believed that this painful conflict was caused by such things as defective loving in childhood, lack of affirmation, conditional approval, etc. As the child develops, its problems are sometimes reinforced by such things as familial tensions, sexual abuse, beatings and emotional put-downs. Not surprisingly, the personality becomes disturbed. It is starved of affirmation and the joy of belonging. Instead, it feels absent from its own depths, and finds it hard to relate satisfactorily to other people, to the world about it, and, ultimately, to God.

Not surprisingly, those who suffer from the inner ache of the heart seek some kind of anaesthetic which will lessen or even deaden their feelings of inadequacy, low self-esteem, stress, shame, alienation etc. Their frustrated desires for loving relationships and a sense of belonging are displaced into unhealthy attitudes and activities. It is this escapist dynamic that leads them to develop process and substance addictions. For example, the alcoholic who has a relationship with his or her bottle has substituted a thing for human intimacy. The addiction is a replacement for the satisfaction of interpersonal needs and a sense of transcendent meaning. Bill Wilson, one of the founders of Alcoholics Anonymous, was such a person. He wrote, 'My self-consciousness was such that I simply had to take my first drink. So I took it, and another one, and then...that strange barrier that existed between me and all men and women seemed to instantly go down. I felt that I belonged where I was, belonging to life, I belonged to the universe; I was part of things at last. Oh, the magic of those first three or four drinks! I became the life of the party...I think, even that first evening, I got thoroughly drunk, and within the next time or two I passed out completely.'[4] Not surprisingly, Bill soon became an alcoholic. Instead of bringing him a sense of happiness, excessive drinking, like any addiction, compounded his problems and increased his sense of misery and isolation.

Research into addictions confirms the fact that many people get involved in them as a result of an understandable but misguided desire to escape from unhappiness. For example, about one in twelve of the adult population suffers from a sex addiction of one kind or another, e.g. compulsive infidelity and child sexual abuse. It has been established that eighty-three per cent of these addicts were themselves sexually abused in childhood, seventy-three per cent were physically abused, and ninety-seven per cent were emotionally abused. Statistics also indicate that sixty-one per cent of the members of Overeating Anonymous come from disturbed, alcoholic families. There is a sad paradox involved in all kinds of addiction. Inner pain drives many people to look for false forms of relief, and their resulting addictions reinforce their sufferings in a way that creates a vicious circle of defeat and shame.

The spiritual effects of addictions

Are addictions sinful? Basically they are illnesses, which can have negative effects from a spiritual point of view. We can look at two of these effects. Firstly, Gerald May makes the interesting observation[5] that addictions are what spiritual writers used to refer to as 'bad habits' and 'attachments'. The word 'attachment' is derived from the old French *atache*, meaning 'nailed to'. In other words, addictions nail down our spiritual desire for transcendent meaning, thereby cutting us off, to a greater or lesser extent, from the experience of God.

Psychologists such as Jung, Frankl, Assagioli and May would concur with St Augustine who asserted that the human heart is restless until it rests in the awareness of the love of God and the God of love. While these well-known doctors of the soul would agree that the desire of addicted people to experience happiness is healthy, they would also say that the way in which they try to satisfy it is not. Unwittingly, it leads to idolatry by making things such as alcohol, pills and work into substitutes for God. Understood in this objective sense, addictions are contrary to the first commandment which says, 'You shall worship the Lord your God and him only shall you serve. You shall have no other gods before me.' As Jesus reminded us, 'you cannot serve God and Mammon' (Mt 6:24). In Philippians 3:19, St Paul informs us that he wept for those whose 'god is the belly' (or for that matter any other created object) and whose 'minds are set on earthly things'.

Secondly, from an objective point of view, addictions such as alcoholism, drug-taking and sex abuse result in grave sin. From a subjective point of view that isn't always the case, due to unconscious influences which lessen the degree of consent. However, these pathological problems can be exploited by the Evil One. He can use them to seduce people into actions that cause serious harm both to themselves and to other people. For example, alcoholics can neglect their primary relationships, tell lies to get out of trouble, steal money to finance their excesses, endanger life by driving under the influence, give bad example to young people, and act in an irresponsible way, perhaps by getting involved in disordered sexual relationships. In Dublin, like many other cities around the world, the rising tide of crime is largely due to the increasing numbers of addicts who need vast sums of money to pay for alcohol and drugs.

The roots of addiction

If we wish to overcome evil, we need to identify our addictions and resolve to give them up. As we know from experience, this is a notoriously difficult thing to do. Before suggesting how we might go about the task, I'd like to mention two approaches that don't work. Clearly, many if not most addictions are the result of neurotic problems. As a result, many addicts try to deal with the emotional causes, by getting involved in counselling and different forms of therapy. Normally, this doesn't work. A few years ago, a member of AA informed me why this is so. He had set up a clinic which helped alcoholics to give up drinking. He said: 'Many of them want therapy in order to get off the booze. But I tell them that until they come off the drink, therapy will do them no good.' More recently, I noticed that Gerald May holds the same opinion. In a book entitled *Care of Mind, Care of Spirit* he writes: 'Attempts to stop dependency through psychotherapy or self-understanding seldom work. Such endeavors have put the cart before the horse. The pattern of chemical abuse must be broken first; then psychotherapy may be in order.'[6]

Addictions usually can't be overcome by means of will-power alone. Perhaps the relatives and friends of addicted people get the mistaken impression that they are weak-willed and lacking a sincere desire to break with their harmful attachments. In reality, many addicts are strong-willed, determined people, who want to stop their particular form of compulsive behaviour. In fact, that is often the essence of their problem. They try to keep their deeper anxieties and conflicts at bay by becoming wilful people who try to exercise too much control in their lives. Time and time again, addicted men and women try to use their considerable will-power to overcome their particular habit. They may succeed for a while. But, before long, they're back to square one. The reason? Their egos are out of touch with their deeper selves. So, while the ego may have the desire to change, it doesn't have the power to do so. That power comes from the self when it is in touch with God. As Gerald May has remarked, 'The agonising cycles of wilfulness and defeat that surround addiction symbolise more than anything else... the fierce line between grace and personal will-power.'[7]

In another of his books, *Will and Spirit*,[8] May contrasts a wilful with a willing attitude to life. Willingness involves a letting go of one's self-separateness, a saying 'yes' to being, an entering into the deepest processes of life, one's own and those of the world. It is a realisation that one is already part of some greater cosmic process. In contrast, wilfulness is setting oneself apart from the fundamental process of life in an attempt to master, direct, control, or otherwise manipulate existence. Wilful people become shipwrecked in their egos. Cut off from the fresh water of their deeper selves they are unable to establish a life-giving sense of connection with the meaning of existence or the mystery of God.

Overcoming addictions

To overcome an addiction, especially when chemical dependency is involved, a number of things is required. Firstly, we
need to notice and admit that we are addicted. Relatives, friends
and colleagues are often painfully aware of the fact, while we go
on denying reality. 'I know I drink,' says an alcoholic, 'but I'm
in control, I could stop any time. After all, last year I was off the
booze for the whole of Lent.' Admittedly, it is easier to acknowledge a chocolate or caffeine addiction than to own up to alcohol
or sex addiction. It has probably to do with the degree of dependency, social stigma and shame involved. That is why the first of
the Twelve Steps to recovery begins by saying: 'We admitted that
we were powerless over...whatever form of addiction afflicts us.'

Secondly, we need to move from *desiring* to give up an addiction, to *wanting* to do so. As a result of smoking heavily for
years, I quickly became addicted to nicotine. I not only admitted that I was hooked, I also recognised that the practice was
bad for my health. So, on many occasions, I resolved to kick the
habit. Like many other smokers, I did so, time and time again.
Then, about twelve years ago, I was living in the chaplain's quar-
ters of an American hospital. To get to my room I had to go
through a ward on the third floor. It was full of men and women
suffering from chest complaints, many of which were the result
of smoking. When I'd hear them coughing, wheezing and gasp-
ing for breath, I'd think, 'If I don't give up the cigarettes, I could
end up in a place like this.' I decided to make yet another effort
to stop smoking. But on this occasion there was something new.
It was the difference between wishing and willing. Whereas in
the past I had *desired* to give up, on this occasion I really *wanted*
to do so. At five minutes to midnight on Shrove Tuesday 1983, I
smoked my last cigarette and, with the help of God, I have never
taken a puff since then.

Thirdly, we need to admit that we are powerless over our
addictions. Instead of us controlling them, they control us. This
is a vital realisation, because it enables the wilful ego to give up
its illusion of control and to open up to the Higher Power which
works in and through the neglected and constricted self. On one
occasion Bill Wilson asked Carl Jung for advice about possible

ways of overcoming alcoholism.[9] The doctor's reply was outlined in an interesting letter. He said that his work with alcoholics had led him to believe that the illness, like many addictions, was a misguided longing for ecstasy. Our English word 'ecstasy' is derived from the Greek *ekstasis* which literally means, 'to stand outside'. In other words, addicted people long to stand outside themselves in order to escape from things like loneliness, fear, inner pain etc. It is not their desire that is questionable, but, rather, their way of satisfying it. Created things, such as alcoholic spirits, are no substitute for the Holy Spirit. 'Alcohol in Latin,' Jung wrote, 'is *spiritus,* and you use the same word for the highest religious experience as well as for the most depraving poison.'[10] He concluded that only a genuine experience of God could rescue people from addiction, by giving them what they needed most, i.e. a deep and abiding sense of belonging. Ephesians 5:18 says much the same, 'Do not get drunk with wine....but be filled with the Spirit.' That is why the second and third of the Twelve Steps to recovery go on to say: 'We came to believe that a power greater than ourselves could restore us to sanity. So we made a decision to turn our will and our lives over to the care of God as we understood Him.'

Bill Wilson discovered that Jung was correct as a result of a personal experience. He had an alcoholic friend called Ebby. On one occasion, when he was hospitalised as a result of his excessive drinking, Bill was visited by Ebby. He noticed that the latter was a changed man. He had given up his drinking as a result of a religious experience which had occurred during a revival meeting some time before. Bill was suitably impressed. A few nights later, he reached his crucifixion point of powerlessness. He was so desperate that he let go of his customary control, surrendered his wilfulness and cried out to the God he didn't yet know, imploring him for help. As someone has rightly said, 'When you hit rock bottom, you sometimes hit the Rock of Ages.'

That is what happened to Bill Wilson. 'Suddenly my room blazed', he wrote, 'with an indescribable white light. I was seized with an ecstasy beyond description....Then, seen in the mind's eye, there was a mountain. I stood upon its summit, where a great wind blew. A wind, not of air, but of spirit. In great, clean strength, it blew right through me. Then came the blazing thought, "You are a free man.".... A great peace stole over me.... I became acutely conscious of a Presence which seemed like a veritable sea of living spirit...."This," I thought, "must be the great reality, the God of the preachers." I seemed to be possessed by the Absolute, and the curious conviction deepened that no matter how wrong things seemed to be, there could be no question of the ultimate rightness of God's universe. For the first time I felt that I really belonged. I knew that I was loved and could love in return.' Sometime later he said, 'Salvation consisted in emerging from isolation to the feeling of being at one with God and man, and to the sense of belonging that came to me. I no longer lived in a completely hostile world. I was no longer frightened and purposeless.'[11] Bill Wilson never took another drink after his spiritual awakening at the age of thirty-nine, in 1934.

Some time after this, Bill Wilson teamed up with Dr Bob, another recovering alcoholic. Together they drew up the famous Twelve Steps listed below.

We:

1. Admitted we were powerless over our addiction, e.g. alcohol, and that our lives had become unmanageable.
2. Came to believe that a power greater than ourselves could restore us to sanity.
3. Made a decision to turn our will and our lives over to the care of God as we understood him.
4. Made a searching and fearless moral inventory of ourselves.
5. Admitted to God, to ourselves, and to another human being the exact nature of our wrongs.
6. Were entirely ready to have God remove all these defects of character.
7. Humbly asked him to remove our shortcomings.
8. Made a list of all persons we had harmed, and became willing to make amends to them all.
9. Made direct amends to such people wherever possible, except when to do so would injure them or others.
10. Continued to take personal inventory and when we were wrong promptly admitted it.

11. Sought through prayer and meditation to improve our conscious contact with God as we understood him, praying only for knowledge of his will for us and the power to carry that out.
12. Having had a spiritual awakening as the result of these steps, we tried to carry this message to addicted people, e.g. alcoholics, and to practice these principles in all our affairs.

While these steps were originally intended to help alcoholics to recover, they have since been adapted, so that people suffering from any kind of addiction can use them to great effect. Nowadays they are used by at least two hundred other groups such as Gamblers Anonymous, Overeaters Anonymous, Sex and Love Addicts Anonymous, Grow Groups, etc.

Steps to complete recovery
To give up an addiction, with the help of the Higher Power of God, is only the beginning of a new beginning. Once the compulsive processes and substance abuse have been brought under control, a lot of work still needs to be done. That is why nine of the twelve steps are devoted to growth and inner healing. There are many good books, such as *Belonging: Bonds of Healing and Recovery* by the Linns, which describe what these steps involve. At this stage, we will look at two concluding points.

Firstly, perhaps the best way of moving from wilfulness to willingness is by developing a contemplative attitude toward oneself, other people, and nature. It means that we pay sustained and self-forgetful attention to reality. We do so by refraining from projecting our own thoughts, theories and interpretations on the objects of our awareness. Instead, we allow them to be themselves, we permit them to reveal and declare their innermost natures to us. As we do so, we will have intimations of the Divine Presence, which is mediated by created reality. We will feel connected to Him, who not only created all things, but who sustains them in being from moment to moment, while loving them all the while. As we do this, our negative images of God will be exposed, challenged and displaced by the Lord of merciful love. For more on this, see the chapter 'Prayer as Attention', in my book *Intimacy and the Hungers of the Heart.*[12]

Secondly, we have seen how the split between the acceptable and unacceptable self, together with the hurts of the years can play a role in the development of our addictions. Having given up our dependencies, Steps Four and Five need to be tackled. By admitting our shameful wrongdoings and omissions to a non-judgemental and loving human being, we can learn to love and accept ourselves as we are, with all our weaknesses. Finally, we need to get in touch with our bad memories and hurts together with their associated feelings and attitudes, in order to bring them to the Lord for his healing. That is the subject of the following chapter. If perchance we have reason to suspect that we are being oppressed by an evil spirit we can go to an experienced Christian to seek his or her discernment and, if needs be, can ask for a prayer for deliverance in a similar way to the one described in chapter 6.

11

INNER HEALING

Nowadays we are familiar with the notion of psychosomatic illness, the fact that physical sicknesses may be connected to one's mental state. For example, it is estimated that about sixty per cent of the problems brought to doctors are stress related. It has been established that chronic stress can be the indirect cause of many health problems, from the common cold to cancer, by inhibiting the effectiveness of the auto-immune system, thereby leaving the person more vulnerable to infection. Over the years I have become increasingly convinced that something similar is involved where sinful thoughts, words, deeds and omissions are concerned. While hurting memories, with their associated negative feelings and attitudes, don't directly cause people to sin, they can do so indirectly, by leaving them particularly vulnerable to illusions, false inspirations and temptations.

Pathology and sin
Over the years I have read the lives of many well-known people. Time and time again, I have been struck by the fact that men and women who come from unhappy families are more likely to become involved in sinful behaviours than those who do not. The life of Joseph Stalin is an example. His father was a rough, violent man who drank heavily and beat his wife and child. Not surprisingly, his behaviour had a bad effect upon his son. A friend, who knew him during his school and college days, commented: 'Undeserved and severe beatings made the boy as hard and heartless as the father was. Since all people in authority over others seemed to him to be like his father, there soon arose in him a vengeful feeling against all people standing above him. From childhood on, the realisation of his thoughts of revenge became the aim to which everything was subordinated.'[1]

As a result of his childhood experiences Stalin developed a narcissistic and paranoid type of personality. His narcissism was apparent in his failure to form normal, healthy relationships with the world around him. Because of his unresolved anxieties, he became self-absorbed and excessively preoccupied with his needs, thoughts, feelings and ambitions. His paranoia was apparent in his propensity to chronic suspicion, jealousy, hypersensitivity, and megalomania. Alice Miller has described the effects of childhood deprivation in this way: 'The repression of our suffering destroys our empathy for the suffering of others....If I as a helpless child was abused and am not allowed to see this, I will abuse other helpless creatures without realising what I am doing.'[2] One could argue that the dreadful crimes for which Stalin was responsible in his adult life, could be explained, at least in part, by his unconscious problems, which he neither acknowledged nor resolved.

Over the years I have visited prisons, counselled troubled people, and heard thousands of confessions. Many of the people who have confided in me were beset with all kinds of problems, ranging from violent behaviour, to compulsive stealing, sexual infidelity, verbal aggression, alcoholism, drug addiction etc. The more I talked with them, the more I realised that although the things they did were objectively wrong, they were often the expressions of unhappy childhoods and traumatic experiences of hurt, in adolescence and adult life. Many of their off-putting and evil actions were rooted in things such as lack of self-acceptance, self-hatred, low self-esteem, separation anxiety, fear of abandonment, and suppressed feelings of hurt, loss, shame, anger, etc.

Over the years I have come to see that painful feelings and conflicts of an unconscious kind have a number of important implications. When assessing the sinfulness of an action, e.g. even something as serious as child sexual abuse, we have to consider two related things. Was the man or woman who engaged in the behaviour consciously aware that it was wrong? Was the action committed with full consent? With regard to the issue of consent, depth psychologists have confirmed an impression shared by many confessors, counsellors, therapists and spiritual directors, that it is sometimes diminished to a greater or lesser extent, by unresolved problems of an unconscious nature. So if we want to turn away from habits of sin we will need to do three interrelated things.

Three ways of turning to the Lord

Firstly, chapter 9 described how we can experience the illuminating, forgiving and strengthening grace of God. The mind is illumined to acknowledge sin. The heart is forgiven through the outpouring of God's merciful love. The will is strengthened in order to resist temptation in the future. While this is the most important step, it needs to be augmented by the two steps below, which deal with the unconscious problems which leave us more vulnerable to temptation. I suspect that it is because these points are often overlooked by penitents and confessors alike, that many people of good will become disheartened. In spite of their intention to do better in the future, they repeatedly fall back into sin. In the end, many of them become so disillusioned that they throw in the towel and stop going to confession altogether. What is needed from a pastoral point of view, is a rediscovery of the healing dimension of the sacrament. As Frank Lake observed in his *Clinical Theology*: 'Pastoral care is defective unless it can deal thoroughly with the evils we have suffered as well as with the sins we have committed.'[3]

Secondly, we can only claim the fullness of Christ's victory over sin when we recover, name and understand our painful memories with their associated feelings and attitudes. As long as the wellsprings of the unconscious mind are infected by negativity, they will continue to contaminate the water of our conscious choices and actions. Despite our good will, we'll end up saying, with St Paul, 'I do not understand my own actions. For I do not do what I want, but I do the very thing I hate' (Rm 7:15).

Thirdly, we will need to bring our painful memories, and their associated feelings and attitudes to the Lord, either privately in prayer, or by revealing them to a trusted friend or confidant, e.g. a priest in the sacrament of reconciliation. Then we can ask the Lord to heal us either directly, or indirectly through the ministry of the other person, so that we grow to have, in the words of Paul, a 'spirit of love, power and self-control' (2 Tm 1:7). Having dealt with the first point in the preceding chapter, I will now go on to examine what is involved in points two and three.

The journey inwards

If we wish to recover, name, understand and express our painful memories, which have been pushed out of sight into the unconscious, we will have to pay attention to our feelings. They are the fingerprints of subjectivity, the point of intersection between our inner lives and the world about us. They not only tell us about our personal reactions to the 'landscape' of external reality, they also reveal a lot about the 'inscape' of our psychological states, conditioned as they are by memories and forgotten influences of all kinds. For example, one priest I met suffered from claustrophobia. It was ruining his ministry. When he was saying Mass the sacristy door had to be kept open. He never heard confessions in a confessional and rarely used public transport. On one occasion he had a panic attack on an aircraft he had just boarded. He had to disembark straight away. Clearly he was suffering from an irrational and embarrassing fear. But why? With the Spirit's help, we eventually uncovered a forgotten memory. When he was three years of age, he had fallen from his father's shoulders into a shallow stream and was nearly drowned. Ever since then, he had been troubled by an unconscious fear of being stifled, choked and suffocated by enclosed spaces. Once that memory and its associated feelings had became conscious, we prayed with success for his inner healing. Freed from his phobia, he was able to carry on his ministry in a normal way.

How do we get in touch with our feelings? Well, firstly we need time on our own, periods when we stop thinking, relax our bodies, and try to become aware of what is going on within. As we do so, we will firstly get in touch with surface feelings such as excitement, sadness, frustration, tension etc. Often these are presenting emotions. There are others which lie beneath them, either in the twilight of the pre-conscious or the darkness of the unconscious mind. Those of a painful and threatening nature are the most significant as far as the subject of inner healing is concerned. Because they are hidden from conscious awareness by efficient defense mechanisms such as rationalisation, repression, projection, introjection, and sublimation, it is difficult to recognise them. Here are a few ways of outmanoeuvering your defence mechanisms, which I have found helpful over the years.

Recovering, naming and understanding feelings

Firstly, ask the Spirit of truth to bring to mind any painful feeling which is preventing you from living a life of wholehearted love. In *Riding the Wind*, George Montague shares the following prophetic advice which he received from the Lord; 'My child, my praise is the only mirror in which you can rightly see yourself and all that is in you. For years you have stood like a sentry at the gate of your dark depths, checking, analysing, and sometimes repressing these things within you. I have been leading you to see that in my presence you must let go of that pretended control and simply pour out my praise. If anxieties, problems or even questionable thoughts or desires surface as you pray, turn them over to me in praise. For as you let them go toward me, you will see their reverse side, you will begin to see their root. Till now you have been cutting off only surface problems – and they have grown back as quickly as you cut. But when you turn totally to me, you can begin to see them totally, and this seeing is the beginning of your healing.'[4]

Secondly, pay attention to your bodily sensations. Is your mouth dry? Are your muscles tense? Have you a headache? Are you perspiring? Communicate with your body, asking it to translate its emotional state into conscious feelings. It will respond in the form of mental images. Feelings always enter consciousness through being connected with some symbolic representation. It is an image of a real or imaginary object that evokes a feeling or is evoked by a feeling; what this means is that there is never a feeling without a symbolic meaning; never a symbol without a feeling. To name one's feelings is to discover the images and symbols that are associated with them. For example, in the course of the day, you recall the image of a weeping person in a late-night movie. For the sake of argument, this could be an indication that you are suffering from an unresolved sense of personal grief and sadness.

It is also important that we remember our dreams. As Freud said, 'they are the royal road to the unconscious'. When the rational mind is off-guard, the psyche uses these night-time videos to express your deepest but most neglected feelings in a symbolic way. When you recall a dream ask yourself these questions. What was the main feeling in the dream? When did I experience that feeling, firstly in the recent and, secondly, in the distant past ?

For example, I dreamt some time ago that I was doing a difficult exam. My main feeling was one of extreme anxiety. I was afraid that I would suffer the shame and embarrassment of failure. When I thought about it, I became more consciously aware of the fact that a few days before, I had been very nervous about an impending interview with my boss. That sense of apprehension, was reminiscent of the the way I had once felt when a teacher sent me to see the intimidating headmistress of my primary school. As far as I can recall, I had to explain why I had broken a boy's front tooth during a fight in the schoolyard. After some further reflection, I became aware of the root of my fears. In childhood, I was scared that I would forfeit the love and approval of my parents, especially my mother, if I failed to live up to their expectations. Ever since then, I have suffered from what is called performance anxiety. Incidentally, it is worth mentioning that as far as the symbolism of dreams is concerned, everyone and everything depicted within them probably represents different aspects of your own personality. So, in my dream, I was obviously the person doing the exam, but the examination itself could have represented the overweening demands of my idealistic, superego self, the satisfaction of which determined my level of self-worth.

Thirdly, we can grow in self-knowledge by talking to people with good listening skills such as friends, trained counsellors or spiritual directors. Because they are more objective, they will be better able to notice our blind spots, evasions, and defenses. As Cassius says to Brutus: 'Since you know you cannot see yourself so well as by reflection, I, your glass, will modestly discover to yourself that of yourself which you yet know not of' (*Julius Caesar*, Act 1 Scene 2). Good listeners help us to grow in self-awareness by helping us to stay with painful emotions which we might otherwise prefer to avoid. Lovingly, they can encourage us to allow such feelings to surface, together with the repressed memories with which they are associated. They can also help us to get beyond bland generalisations such as, 'I felt bad when my father used to shout at my mother,' to being more specific: 'I felt terrified when my father used to shout in a loud and aggressive way at my mother. I wanted to protect her, but I didn't know what to do. I felt ashamed of my passivity and powerlessness.' I may say in passing that sometimes the Holy Spirit will enable gifted Christians to get intuitive hunches about repressed memories of a painful kind. For example, he or she could sense that a depressed woman had been traumatised, as a twelve-year-old, by her mother's sudden death. Her current problems are probably due to the fact that she has repressed her acute sense of loss and never dealt with her unconscious feelings of grief.

As we get in touch with forgotten feelings and memories of a painful kind, we can try to understand the root issues involved. For example, John Bradshaw, a well-known therapist and writer, has said that in twenty-two years of working with addicted people, he had 'never seen anyone who did not have abandonment issues and internalised shame, along with their physical addiction.'[5]

In my experience there are other common problems of a recurring kind, such as:

– An unresolved sense of loss, sadness and grief.
– Repressed anger, due to the fact that one's parents wouldn't tolerate it, and which in adult life has tended to turn into anxiety and depression.
– Feelings of insecurity and fear which are rooted in separation anxiety that first emerged in the early years of life as a result of experiencing parental love of a conditional kind
– Feelings of worthlessness, inadequacy, shame and not belonging.
– Feelings of bitterness, resentment and vengefulness.
– A sense of meaninglessness, apathy, and sometimes despair.

Unchristian emotional attitudes

Feelings like these, which were first evoked in childhood, can go on to consolidate into emotional attitudes, i.e. permanent and consistent ways of responding to reality in a prejudiced way. For example, in his book *Inner Healing*, Michael Scanlan mentions five such attitudes.[6] (I'm sure there are many others.)

1. A judgemental spirit that is harsh and demanding on self and others.

2. A perfectionist attitude that demands the impossible from oneself and others.
3. A strong propensity to fear future events.
4. A feeling of aloneness, abandonment and dejection during times of decision-making.
5. A preoccupation with one's own guilt and a tendency to compete for status and success, often in an unscrupulous way.

While feelings are neither right or wrong, I believe that some emotional attitudes such as self-hatred, resentment and pessimism are sinful from an objective, if not always from a subjective point of view. But once we identify them, and acknowledge that they are neither in harmony with revealed truth, or the will of God, we need to repent of them, in the way described in chapter 9.

Clearly, if our hurts have led us to become bitter and resentful we need to forgive those who have hurt us. I would say without hesitation that inner healing will elude us until we forgive those who have hurt us, from our hearts. If you want to forgive someone you could use the following method.

A. Imagine the person you desire to forgive, standing in front of you.
B. See him or her illumined by the converging beams of God's mercy and love. Acknowledge that the Lord loves that person in the same unconditional way that he loves you.
C. Now, say the following prayer or something like it. 'In the name of our Lord Jesus Christ, who loves us and died for the forgiveness of our sins, I forgive you from the bottom of my heart for the hurt that you have caused me. I call down God's blessing upon you, and thank God that you are now forgiven. Amen.' The word 'amen' means 'let it be so, I believe that it is accomplished.'

If in the future your hurting and resentful feelings bubble up again, affirm in faith that they have no real power. Feelings aren't facts. The truth is, you are standing in the grace of divine forgiveness. However, some hurts go so deep that they cannot be easily or quickly forgiven. Like an onion that is being peeled, one layer of hurt only reveals another. And so forgiveness has to come in instalments. Perhaps this is the implication of Jesus' saying that we should forgive 'seventy times seven times' (Mt 18:22).

The healing of memories

Once we have recovered, named and understood the origin and effects of our painful feelings we can go on to express them. There are a number of ways of doing this.

1. The simplest way is to write about your feelings and experiences in a personal journal. This is a good start because it will help you to be more objective about your experience.
2. Sharing your painful feelings and memories with a friend or confidant is even better.
3. What is even better still, is to tell the Lord the truth, the whole truth and nothing but the truth about your sufferings, while remembering Luther's adage, 'Prayer is not tellings lies to God.'

As you express your hurting emotions and bruised memories in these ways, you can expect to experience the healing and strengthening Spirit of the Lord. For example, there is abundant evidence to show that when we share our troubled emotions with an empathic person it can have a healing effect. The following story illustrates the point. Tom worked as a nurse's aide in a psychiatric hospital. The sickest person in that hospital was a psychotic woman who had been there for eighteen years. In all that time she had never spoken to anyone. All day long she sat in a rocking chair and moved back and forth. The doctors tried to help her, but without success. Tom noticed this unfortunate woman. He found another rocking chair and pulled it over next to hers. That evening, during his meal break, he brought his dinner, sat in the chair and rocked beside the woman as he ate. He returned the next evening and the next. He even came in on his days off. In fact, he came every evening for six months and rocked beside the woman. She never responded. Finally, one evening, as Tom was getting up to leave, the woman looked him straight in the eye and said, 'Good night, Tom.' After that, she began to get well. Tom still came each evening and rocked beside her. Eventually she recovered completely and was released from the hospital.

You will find that the same can be true for you. As you share your hurting self in a humble and trusting way, the understanding, acceptance and love of your friend or confidant will be used by the Spirit to bring you inner healing. If needs be, you can ask, either that person, or someone with a healing ministry, to pray for you, that out of God's glorious riches, 'he may strengthen you with power through his Spirit in your inner being' (Ep 3:16).

As you share your burden with the Lord in prayer, you can ask him for a healing of your memories. He may answer your request directly and privately, or indirectly through the power of the sacraments of reconciliation, anointing and the Eucharist, which bring us, in the words of the liturgy, 'health of mind and body'. I have met a number of people over the years who, by the grace of God, have experienced sacramental healing of debilitating fears, mind-numbing depressions and unresolved feelings of worthlessness.

12

RESISTING TEMPTATION

Genesis describes how, from the very beginning of time, people were tempted by the Evil One. The gospels show how, from the beginning of his public ministry, Jesus was also 'tempted by the Devil' (Mt 4:1). After his three encounters with Satan, we are told that he 'departed from him for a while' (Lk 4:13). Clearly, the prince of darkness was going to return time and time again, especially during Passion week. Therefore, Hebrews 4:15 can say with good reason, 'we have one who has been tempted in every way that we are but without sinning.' The truth is, temptation is a universal phenomenon; no one, not even Jesus, was exempt. 'No temptation has overtaken you, that it is not common to everyone', says St Paul in 1 Corinthians 10:13.

Our English words 'tempt' and 'temptation' are derived from the Latin *temptare,* which means 'to test,' or 'to try the strength of something'. In theology we say that while God may test a person's fidelity by allowing him or her to endure all kinds of trials, tribulations, and temptations, he never tempts them himself. As scripture says, 'No one when tempted should say, "I am being tempted by God," for God cannot be tempted by evil, and he himself tempts no one' (Jm 1:13).

Two sources of temptation

Temptation can have two sources. The first is rooted in our own sinful desires: 'One is tempted by one's own desire, being lured and enticed by it, then when that desire has conceived, it gives birth to sin' (Jm 1:14). For example, St Paul says, 'Those who want to be rich fall into temptation and are trapped by many senseless and harmful desires that plunge people into ruin and destruction. For the love of money is a root of all kinds of evil' (1 Tm 6:9-10).

There is, however, a second source of temptation. In Revelation 12:17 we are told, in mythological images how, having being cast out of heaven as a result of his pride, the Devil 'went off to make war' on those of God's children who try to keep his commandments. St Peter says that 'he prowls around like a roaring lion, seeking someone to devour' (1 P 5:8). In the *Summa Theologiae*, St Thomas Aquinas confirms this view,[1] when he says that the proper role of the Devil is to tempt. Later in this chapter we will look at some of the ways in which he does this.

Lead us not into temptation

In the Lord's Prayer, Jesus taught us to say, 'lead us not into temptation, but deliver us from evil.' There has been a lot of discussion about the exact meaning of these petitions. At first sight they seem to imply that, contrary to what James has said, God does tempt us to find out how faithful and committed we really are. In the *Catechism of the Catholic Church* this dilemma is resolved.[2] It points out that it is hard to translate the Greek verb 'to tempt' with an appropriate English word. It can mean 'do not allow us to enter into temptation', and also 'do not let us yield to temptation'. In other words, we ask the Lord not to allow us to take the way that leads to sin. The Catechism also has an interesting observation to make about the phrase, 'deliver us from evil'. 'In this petition,' it says, 'evil is not an abstraction, but refers to a person, Satan, the Evil One, the angel who opposes God. The Devil is the one who "throws himself across" God's plan and his work of salvation accomplished in Christ.'

Given the fact that temptation, like trials and tribulations, is an inevitable aspect of human life, it is important to stress the fact that it can have a very positive effect. For example, Origen (c.185-c.254) was one of the greatest thinkers in the early Church. He wrote, 'No one but God knows what our soul has received from him, not even we ourselves. But temptation reveals it in order to teach us to know ourselves, and in this way we discover our evil inclinations and are obliged to give thanks for the good that temptation has revealed to us.'[3] St Augustine echoed this point when he said in *The City of God*, 'For the most part, the human mind cannot attain to self-knowledge unless it explores its power through temptation, by some kind of experience and not merely verbal self-questioning.' In our own time

Jung said something similar when he remarked that there is no growth in consciousness without painful trials and struggles.

How to resist temptation

As was already noted, we have the assurance of scripture that we will be able to resist the temptations that emanate both from our own human natures and from the Evil One. As St Paul said, 'No testing has overtaken you that is not common to man. God is faithful, and he will not let you be tempted beyond your strength, but with every temptation will also provide the way of escape, so that you may be able to endure it' (1 Co 10:13). While this is true, it presupposes that the person is spiritually mature, humble, realistic, self-aware and deeply committed to God. Because that isn't always the case, many people, despite their good intentions, do fall into sin. The evil they wish to avoid is the very thing that they do (Rm 7:19).

There is an interesting example of this dilemma in the gospels. Peter loved Jesus. He promised to go to Jerusalem and, if necessary, to die with him. But Jesus knew his friend through and through. He responded, 'Simon, Simon, listen! Satan has sought permission to sift all of you like wheat, but I have prayed for you that your own faith may not fail; and you, when once you have turned back, strengthen your brothers' (Lk 22:31-33). Jesus knew that Satan would exploit Peter's weakness during Passion week. Surprisingly, he didn't pray that he would overcome temptation. The Lord knew a fall was inevitable, because Peter's spiritual life had been built on the sand of presumption and lack of self-awareness. So he prayed instead, that when Peter had fallen, he wouldn't be so filled with self-contempt that, like Judas, he would doubt God's mercy and love. In fact, Peter's fall not only taught him a lot about himself and the power and tactics of the Evil One, it also evoked a heartfelt desire for an outpouring of the Spirit, one that was gloriously fulfilled at Pentecost.

In retrospect he would have been able to say of his sin, 'O happy fault, O necessary sin, that gained for me such a wonderful blessing...where sin abounded in my life, the grace of God has more abounded' (Rm 11:32). Pope John Paul I adverted to this paradox when he said, 'I run the risk of making a blunder, but I will say it: the Lord loves humility so much that he sometimes allows serious sins. Why? In order that those who committed them may, after repenting, remain humble. One does not feel oneself inclined to think oneself half a saint, half an angel, when one knows that one has committed serious faults.' It could be added that, having sinned, we not only learn about our vulnerability and weaknesses, we also learn from personal experience how to recognise the typical manoeuvres of the Evil One.

In chapter 7 we saw how St Ignatius believed that the Devil tries to separate people from the Lord, not by tempting them to commit what are obviously serious sins, but in a more subtle way. He begins by tempting people to have an inordinate and idolatrous desire for riches, reputation, and eventually ethical autonomy. It is at this stage in particular that subjectivist views of right and wrong can lead people into serious, but often unacknowledged sin. In his Spiritual Exercises[4] St Ignatius says that in order to resist temptation we need to be familiar with the the Devil's tactics. Typically, he likes to operate as a bully who intimidates, a seducer who likes secrecy, or as a military commander who exploits our principal weaknesses. I will look at each tactic in turn, while suggesting how best to overcome it.

The bully who intimidates

The Devil comes on strong during temptation. He tries to intimidate us in order to produce a resigned defeatism in the heart. The weaker the person appears to be, the more the Devil will try to bully him or her by piling on the pressure. But if, from the onset of the temptation, the person is firm and courageous in resisting his promptings, the Devil is exposed as a coward. St Ignatius writes, 'It is the custom of the enemy to become weak, lose courage and turn to flight with his seductions as soon as one leading a spiritual life faces temptations boldly, and does exactly the opposite of what the enemy suggests. However, if one begins to be afraid and to lose courage in temptations, no wild animal on earth can be more fierce than the enemy of our human nature.'[5] This advice is particularly relevant during times of desolation, when the inner sense of God's presence can be eclipsed and we are troubled by feelings like restlessness, aridity, sadness and hopelessness. It is just when we are at our lowest ebb that the enemy will attack. It is then, too, that we need to recall that 'the spirit you received is not a spirit of cowardice, but rather a spirit of power ...and self-control...so resist the Devil and he will flee from you' (2 Tm 1:7; Jm 4:7). The great spiritual writers counsel that it is important to resist temptation as soon as it begins. Thomas à Kempis wrote: 'We must be watchful, especially in the beginning of temptation, because it is then that the enemy is more easily overcome if he is not allowed to come in through the door of the soul, but instead is kept out and resisted from his first knock....Withstand the beginning, after-remedies come too late.'[6]

The seducer who likes secrecy

The Evil One likes to work in secret. Like a married man who has seduced a young woman, or vice versa, he will urge the person he tempts not to tell confessors, friends or confidants about his temptations. He will suggest that this is the best policy either because they wouldn't understand, or because they would be too harsh, too busy, or too lax. 'He knows,' says Ignatius, 'that he cannot succeed in his evil undertaking once his evident deceits have been revealed....But if one reveals them to a good confessor or a spiritual person with knowledge of such deceits and malicious intentions, the Evil One will be quite vexed, knowing that it cannot succeed in this evil undertaking once its obvious deceptions have been revealed.'[7] So, in time of temptation, it is a prudent thing to reveal one's struggle, no matter how shameful or embarrassing it might be, to a person who is experienced in the area of discernment of spirits. St Vincent de Paul once wrote, 'If anyone feels troubled by ideas which seem to be in some way misleading, or upset by acute anxiety or temptation, he should tell a spiritually experienced person, such as a spiritual director, so that the matter can be competently dealt with.'[8]

The military commander who exploits weakness

The Devil is like a good military commander. He exploits a person's greatest vulnerability, especially during times of desolation. 'The enemy of our human nature,' says Ignatius, 'explores from every side all our virtues of intellect, faith and morals. Where he finds our defences weakest and most deficient in regard to eternal salvation, it is at that point that the enemy attacks, trying to overcome us by storm.'[9] Psychologists have always suggested that each personality type has a characteristic weakness. For example, those with a sanguine temperament are inclined to sensuality; those with a melancholic temperament incline to sadness and depression; those with a choleric temperament incline to anger and insensitivity; and those with a phlegmatic temperament incline to apathy and laziness. Devotees of the Enneagram maintain that there are nine personality types. Each one is said to have a characteristic blind spot or obsession, e.g. an inordinate desire to avoid anger, pain, a sense of need, failure, ordinariness, emptiness, non-conformity, vulnerability and conflict.

If a person is insecure, inwardly divided between the acceptable and unacceptable self, and suffering from unresolved conflicts and negative emotions, he or she will be even more vulnerable to temptation. For example, when the ego, i.e. the executive part of the personality, is lacking confidence and authority, there are often repressed and unacknowledged feelings such as anxiety, anger, guilt and resentment. As a result the person may feel lonely, isolated and demoralised. At this point, what Freud called the 'id', i.e. the amoral, instinctual side of the unconscious, will stimulate a desire for revitalisation by means of sensual pleasure, often of a sexual kind. It can well up within the personality as a physical urge or as a seductive erotic fantasy. Needless to say, the Devil can exploit psychological processes like these to tempt people to sin. That is why mature Christians need the kind of self-awareness that recognises where the protection is most needed. Otherwise they will be caught unawares. Afterwards they may confess in dismay, 'I don't know what came over me...it wasn't like me to do something like that.' Once we grow in self-knowledge, however, we will know from personal experience which occasions of sin we most need to avoid.

Prayer and temptation

There is an Irish proverb which says that the day of the wind is not the day to thatch a house. In terms of this chapter, it means that we need to build up our spiritual strength when we have the opportunity, so that we may have the power to resist in the day of testing and temptation. Spiritual writers have always maintained that the fervent prayer of the heart was particularly helpful in this regard.

In the course of his agony in the garden of Gethsemane, Jesus said to his sleepy apostles, 'Stay awake and pray that you will not fall into temptation, the spirit indeed is willing, but the flesh is weak' (Mt 26:41). In a well-known conference on prayer,[10] Abbott Cassian (360-435) provided sage and useful advice in this regard. He wanted to provide his followers with a simple method of centreing prayer, one that would enable them to pray always, and to find help in all their needs. He said that the Fathers of the Desert believed that no matter what insight a person received as a result of reading and meditating on the scriptures, it could be summed up in the scriptural verse, 'O God, come to my assistance, Lord make haste to help me' (Ps 70:1).

Incidentally, Eastern Christians use the Jesus prayer instead, i.e. 'Lord, Jesus Christ, Son of the living God, have mercy on me, a sinner.' Speaking of any invocation like this Cassian said: 'It fits every mood of human nature, every temptation, every circumstance. It contains an invocation of God, a humble confession of faith, a reverent watchfulness, a meditation upon our frailty, a confidence in God's answer, an assurance of his ever-present support.'[11] Cassian went on to say, 'The mind should go on grasping this formula until it can cast away the wealth and multiplicity of other thoughts and restrict itself to the poverty of this single verse.' In this way a person becomes poor in spirit. 'Such a one,' he comments, 'truly confesses himself a beggar of the Lord, like the psalmist who said, 'I am a beggar and a poor man: and God helps me' (Ps 40:17).[12]

This kind of prayer can have a number of effects. To begin with, Cassian was of the opinion that it would enable the mind to attain the purest form of contemplation, one that would transcend the limitations of images and concepts, to enjoy loving union with the mystery of God. A Russian Orthodox bishop, Brianchaninov, has succinctly described how this form of prayer brings about sobriety of heart, i.e. detachment, recollection and purity of intention. 'It is one thing,' he says, 'to pray with attention with the participation of the heart; it is another thing to descend with the mind into the temple of the heart and from there to offer mystical prayer filled with divine grace and power. The second is the result of the first. The attention of the mind during prayer draws the heart into sympathy. With the strengthening of the attention, sympathy of the heart and mind is turned into union of heart and mind. Finally, when attention makes the prayer its own, the mind descends into the very heart for the most profound and secret service of prayer.'[13] People who are used to praying always in this way, are well prepared to cope with temptation. As soon as it occurs, they can resort with expectant faith to the prayer formula, e.g. 'O God, come to my assistance, Lord, make haste to help me.' As they do, they will be enabled to resist temptation, no matter how strong or persistent it might be.

Self-denial and temptation

We have noted in earlier chapters, how our sinful desires originate in the old, self-centred nature that can be traced back to our first parents. Principal among these, is a tendency to indulge ourselves in sensual gratifications such as eating and drinking, and sexual activities of one kind or another etc. Although these things can be good in themselves, we know from experience that they can become the source of temptation and sin. To counteract their influence we need to engage in sensible self-denial by means of asceticism.

The word 'asceticism' comes from the Greek meaning, 'to train or to discipline.' It has the world of sport in mind, where men and women engage in rigorous and sometimes painful exercises in order to become fit and strong. St Paul refers to this when he says, 'Athletes exercise self-control in all things; they do it to receive a perishable wreath, but we an imperishable one. So I do not run aimlessly, nor do I box as though beating the air: but I punish my body and enslave it, so that after proclaiming the good news to others I should not be disqualified' (1 Co 9:25-26).

We can curb and counteract the selfish, self-indulgent inclinations of our natures, by engaging in such things as voluntary fasting and almsgiving. We can also renounce satisfactions, sensual, imaginative and intellectual, which may not be sinful in themselves. In this way the spiritual self is strengthened. When temptation comes, we are better able to resist it, with the help of the Lord. As Jesus said to the apostles when they asked him why they hadn't been able to overcome the influence of the Evil One, 'This kind can only be overcome through prayer and fasting [i.e. acts of self-denial]' (Mk 9:29).

13

DISCERNMENT OF SPIRITS

What is the central ethical teaching of the New Testament? I suppose a number of texts could be nominated, such as 'Thy will be done on earth, as it is in heaven' (Mt 6:10), or 'Love your neighbour as yourself' (Rm 13:9). However, I have believed for some time that any possible contenders can be summed up in the phrase, 'live in the Spirit,' or be 'guided by the Spirit' (Ga 5:16, 18). Commenting on this verse, scripture scholar George Montague has said that it is theological dynamite.[1] The Christian life is not a list of do's and don'ts. It is the gift of being moved by the Spirit of God, and the key to holiness is to allow the Spirit to lead. Paul clearly speaks of ethical values and practical actions which are based on inspiration. It is not reserved for exceptionally holy people but is readily available to all who believe in Christ. When confronted with any moral decision, great or small, ideally the Christian's first question would be, 'Where does the Spirit lead me in this?' Speaking about divine guidance St Vincent de Paul said, 'Temptation is an impulse turning us toward something evil and inspiration is another impulse turning us toward good. The Devil brings us to evil through temptation and God brings us to good through inspiration.'[2]

Those who want to be led by the Spirit would be well advised to say the following prayer at the beginning of each day. It was attributed to Cardinal Newman and later adapted by Cardinal Mercier, who promised that those who used it would be richly blessed. 'O, Holy Spirit, soul of my soul, I adore you. Enlighten, guide, strengthen and console me. I promise to be submissive in all that you ask of me, and to accept all that you allow to happen to me. Just show me your holy will.'[3] In many of the circumstances of our lives the will of God is pretty clear. It is expressed in the teachings of scripture, e.g. the Ten Commandments; and in the laws of the Church, e.g. those about artificial forms of contraception. But, day by day, opportunities arise and decisions have to be made which are not covered by either. In circumstances such as these, we need to work out for ourselves what it is that God wants us to do.

Guidance from the Holy Spirit

The Lord normally offers us his guidance during our prayer times. As St Vincent de Paul once said, 'Prayer is a conversation of the heart with God, a mutual communication in which God inwardly tells the person what he wishes him to do and in which the person tells his God what He Himself has taught him to ask for....So, establish a close union between yourself and our Lord in prayer. That is the reservoir from which you will receive all the inspirations you need....When in doubt, turn to God and say to him: 'O Lord, you are the Father of light, teach me what I ought to do in these circumstances.' I give you this advice, not only to help you in those difficulties which will cause you pain, but also that you may learn directly from God what he wants you to do.'[4] In a chapter on guidance in *Maturing in the Spirit*,[5] I describe some of the ordinary and charismatic ways in which God can direct our lives. At this point I will mention just three of them.

Firstly, when we become aware of who God is and what he is like, he seems to say to our hearts: 'Be for others what I am for you.' So, if in prayer you found him to be compassionate, accepting, forgiving, understanding, non-judgemental etc., then be compassionate, accepting, forgiving, understanding and non-judgemental in your dealings with others. Secondly, a line of scripture may have been dead on the page as far as you were concerned. Suddenly, by God's grace it jumps alive into your heart as an inspired word of guidance, e.g. telling you not to be afraid, to reverence the poor, to forgive and love an enemy, etc. Thirdly, the Holy Spirit can prompt all kinds of holy desires and inspirations in your heart. They can manifest themselves in the form of thoughts, feelings, images, impulses and the like. When you, or anyone else appears to receive guidance in this way, you need to discern whether it is truly prompted by the Lord. For, as St Ignatius of Loyola has pointed out, 'There are three kinds of thought in the mind, namely: one which is strictly my own, and

97

arises wholly from my own free will; two others which come from without, the one from the good Spirit, the other from the Evil One.'[6]

Types of discernment

The inspired writers of the scriptures were well aware that the 'enemy of our souls' could appear as an 'angel of light' (2 Co 11:14). He could lead people astray by means of illusions and false inspirations. As a result, discernment of spirits was necessary. 'Test everything,' wrote St Paul, 'retain what is good. Refrain from every evil' (1 Th 5:19-22). St John added, 'Beloved, do not trust every spirit but test the spirits to see whether they belong to God, because many false prophets have gone out into the world' (1 Jn 4:1). Speaking of those who came to receive inspiration as a result of a religious experience, Pope Paul VI had this to say: 'Prudence. Here opens one of the most difficult and complex chapters of the spiritual life, that of the "discernment of spirits". Misunderstandings are very easy in this field; illusion no less so.'[7] It seems to me that there are possibly three forms of 'testing', or discernment. However, the first two, as we shall see, may be so interrelated as to become almost one.

The charism of discernment

Firstly, in 1 Corinthians 12:10, St Paul mentions the charism of discernment of spirits. In his commentary on this text, scripture scholar George Montague maintains[8] that it is a Spirit-given ability to recognise whether a prophecy which is uttered by somebody in the community is truly from the Lord or not. For example, at charismatic prayer meetings people will occasionally claim that God has given them a word either for the group or for the wider church. Indeed, the same claim is sometimes made by people who maintain that our Lady, or an angel, has given them a message, e.g. the visionaries at the Melleray Grotto, Cappoquin, Co. Waterford in 1985. A person endowed with a genuine charism of discernment might sense whether such messages were inspired by the Lord or not. In the modern charismatic movement, however, the charism of discernment is normally understood in a wider sense, as an ability to assess the authenticity of any inspiration, charismatic or otherwise. If the charism of discernment is understood in this second, wider sense, then it would probably merge into the following form.

Connatural discernment

Secondly, there is what is known technically as connatural discernment. It is rooted in the gifts of wisdom and knowledge mentioned in Isaiah 11:2, and enables some people to have an instinctive sense of what is divinely inspired. St Thomas wrote in the *Summa Theologiae*: 'To judge well about the things of God....through a certain oneness in nature with God is an act of the Spirit's gift of wisdom. Such sympathy or connaturality with divine things is an effect of the love of charity uniting us to God, so that wisdom's cause is love in the will, even if in essence wisdom is a disposition of mind to judge well. The gift of understanding guides the mind's perceptions, but the gifts of wisdom and knowledge form its judgements.'[9] Thomist scholar Garrigou-Legrange has written, by way of explanation, 'As the bee or carrier pigeon is directed by instinct, and acts with a wonderful certainty revealing the Intelligence which directs them, just so, says St Thomas, the spiritual person is inclined to act, not principally through the movement of his own will, but by the instinct of the Holy Spirit.'[10] This seems to me to be the most common form of discernment among devout Christians. For example, in everyday life, if you know someone very well, it only takes a micro-second, a syllable of speech, to distinguish his or her voice from that of anyone else who might phone you. It is much the same for people who enjoy a close personal relationship with Jesus. When they receive an inspiration, they can distinguish the voice of the Lord from any other. As a result, they have an intuitive sense of what is good or bad, right or wrong, true or false, Godly or un-Godly.

Isn't this what Jesus promised when he said, 'The Spirit will lead you into all truth' (Jn 16:13)? We can note in passing that this point finds an echo in at least three other New Testament texts. The first says, 'As for you, the anointing that you received from God abides in you, and so you do not need anyone to teach you as this anointing teaches you all things' (1 Jn 2:17).

The second adds, 'I will put my laws in their minds, and write them on their hearts' (Hb 8:10). Finally, the third assures us that 'What no eye has seen, nor ear heard, nor the human heart conceived...God has revealed to us through the Spirit; for the Spirit searches everything even the depths of God...(so) we have the mind of Christ' (1 Co 2:9-10;16).

Pope John Paul II has written about this kind of inspiration in *Veritatis Splendor* (n. 64). Although it is a bit difficult to understand at first reading, it is worth quoting at some length. 'It is the "heart" converted to the Lord and to the love of what is good which is really the source of true judgements of conscience. Indeed, in order to "prove what is the will of God, what is good and acceptable and perfect" (Rm 12:2), knowledge of God's law in general is necessary, but it is not sufficient: what is essential is a sort of "connaturality" between man and the true good. Such a connaturality is rooted in and develops through the virtuous attitudes of the individual himself: prudence and the other cardinal virtues, and even before these the theological virtues of faith, hope and charity. This is the meaning of Christ's saying: "He who does what is true comes into the light" (Jn 3:21).'

The art of discernment

Thirdly, there is the art of discernment. Instead of relying solely on a charismatic gift or an intuitive ability, this experiential approach is based on a traditional way of assessing religious inspirations. It can be traced back to early Church Fathers such as Evagarius and Cassian. How can we judge whether an inspiration comes from God or not? Mindful that Jesus said, 'by their fruits you shall know them' (Mt 7:16), can we judge by looking at external actions? In other words, if an action is good in itself, e.g. doing voluntary work for the homeless, can we presume that the inspiration that prompted such action came from God? We can arrive at an answer by looking at the parable of the Pharisee and the tax collector.

It is obvious that the religious official was leading a very good life from an external point of view. He spoke the truth when he said, 'I thank you that I am not like all other men – robbers, evil-doers, adulterers, – or even like this tax collector. I fast twice a week and give a tenth of my income.' But Jesus wasn't impressed. Despite his good actions, the Pharisee suffered from an off-putting dose of inner pride and conceit. The tax collector, on the other hand, led a bad life from the outward point of view. But inwardly, at least he was honest and humble before the Lord. And so, despite his bad actions, Jesus says that he went home in a better spiritual state than the Pharisee. If we cannot base discernment of spirits on external fruits such as good actions, what can we base it on?

The traditional answer can be traced back to the teaching of Jesus when he maintained that it was the intention of the heart that determined what was good or bad. 'Do not keep judging,' he advised, 'according to outward appearances; let your judgement be according to what is right' (Jn 7:24). At another time he said, 'Words flow out of what fills the heart' (Mt 15:19), and again, 'From the heart come evil intentions: murder, adultery, fornication, theft, perjury, slander' (Mt 12:34). So, rather than looking at external actions, the art of discernment examines inner inspirations while trying to establish their origin and orientation. Do they come from God, the self or even the Evil One? Do they lead the person toward, or away from a deeper, more committed relationship to God?

Unlike those evangelical and charismatic fundamentalists, who sometimes espouse a dualistic view, the Catholic tradition has always believed that rather than coming from either God or the Evil One, many if not most of our inspirations come from the human heart. And that heart, as Jeremiah 17:9 reminds us, 'is devious above all else; it is perverse – who can understand it?' In contemporary language we could say that the unconscious mind, especially its darker side, can exert a large but unacknowledged influence upon our conscious intentions. For example, the person who is inspired to help the homeless, could be motivated by an unconscious feeling of resentment and guilt, or by a desire to appear to be charitable in his own eyes or the eyes of others.

Consolation and desolation

Over the centuries, spiritual writers like St Ignatius of Loyola, have come to see that if an inspiration is prompted by God, it will be associated with inner consolation, i.e. fruits of the Spirit, such as the joy and peace which are mentioned in Galatians 5:22. When an inspiration has not been prompted by God, it will tend to lead to inner desolation. St Vincent de Paul has written, that 'a mark of illusions and false inspirations is that they are persistent and troublesome and make us uneasy,'[11] whereas the ones that come from God 'instil themselves gently into our souls and incline us to seek whatever concerns the greater glory of God.' Speaking of the difference between consolation and desolation St Ignatius wrote: 'Desolation is the contrary to consolation. Contrary to peace there is conflict; contrary to joy, sadness: contrary to hope in higher things, hope in base things; contrary to heavenly love, earthly love; contrary to tears, dryness; contrary to elevation of mind, wandering of mind to contemptible things.'[12]

In his autobiography, Ignatius describes how he first noticed this distinction. When he was recovering from a war wound he was aware of two strong desires. The first was evoked when he read lives of Christ and the saints. They filled him with a longing to do great things for God. The second was evoked by the thought of an attractive woman at court. He desired to serve her as her knight. He noticed that while he entertained each of these desires he experienced consolation. However, as soon as he stopped thinking of the lady at court 'he was dry and discontented.' On the other hand, when he stopped thinking of imitating Christ and the saints, 'he remained happy and content.' Ignatius goes on to tell us, 'He began to marvel at the difference and to reflect upon it, realising from experience that some thoughts left him sad and others happy. Little by little he came to recognise the difference between the spirits that influenced him, one from the demon, the other from God.'[13]

Worldly and holy desires

It is worth noting the fact that St Ignatius felt in the last analysis all our promptings and inspirations could be boiled down to two kinds of desire. In an earlier chapter, we noted that in a qualified sense we have two natures. The unredeemed self, which can be traced back to Adam, is egocentric and worldly in nature. The redeemed self, which can be traced back to Jesus, the New Adam, is God-centred and spiritual in nature. Desires of a worldly kind emanate from the unredeemed self, e.g. a longing for riches, reputation and ethical autonomy. Desires of a spiritual nature are prompted in the heart by God, e.g. a longing to have an intimate knowledge of our Lord, who has become human for us, so that we may love him more dearly, and follow him more nearly. These desires are in conflict, for as St Paul has noted, 'What the flesh desires is opposed to the Spirit, and what the Spirit desires is opposed to the flesh; for these desires are opposed to each other, to try to prevent you from doing what you want' (Ga 5:17).

To be guided by the Spirit, therefore, we need to be consciously aware of our spiritual desires. Over the years I have noticed that we can lose touch with them for any one of three reasons.

- Firstly, they can lie buried beneath the debris of our worldly desires. As Jesus said, 'worries about this life, the love of riches, and all kinds of other desires crowd in and choke (them)' (Mk 4:17).
- Secondly, many Christians suffer from hardening of the 'oughteries.' They find it hard to get beyond the 'oughts, shoulds, musts and have to's' of a legalistic sense of obligation, to become aware of the 'needs, yearnings, wants, and desires' of personal conviction.
- Thirdly, unrecognised and unresolved feelings of hurt, loss and conflict etc., can be so distracting as to eclipse the serene light of spiritual desire.

Not surprisingly, therefore, discernment of spirits requires a certain degree of self-awareness, an honest acknowledgment of the factors that may be separating us from the deeper, Spirit-prompted desires of the heart. These desires can be evoked by inspired thoughts, images, values, ideals, beliefs, etc. For example, for one reason or another, you might want to get involved in an adult education course, to have no more children, or to buy a bigger and better house. If your desire has been prompted by the Spirit, it will be associated with consolation rather than desolation of spirit. St Ignatius warns,[13] however, that if you are enduring a time of desolation because God has withdrawn his consolation from you – in order to test your commitment to him and to purify your will and motivations – you won't be in a position to verify whether your promptings and inspirations are coming from God or not. As Ignatius is alleged to have said, people who make a big life decision during a time of desolation, e.g. to separate from a spouse, or give all their money to the poor, may have the Devil as their spiritual director. Such decisions should be postponed until consolation of spirit returns.

The examen of consciousness

The whole subject of discernment of spirits is subtle and complex. I have only mentioned some of the basic points in this chapter. Before concluding, I have one more practical suggestion. You can grow in the ability to discern good from bad spirits by conducting what is known as an examen of consciousness – as distinct from an examination of conscience – at the end of each day. It is a way of tuning in to one's experience, specifically those feelings of consolation and desolation which were associated with the inspirations, decisions and actions of the day. You may find that the following method is helpful.

1. Affirm in faith that God is present.
2. Consider these words of Cardinal Newman:
   'God's inspirations are not discerned at the time they are upon us, but afterwards when we look back upon what is gone and over.'
3. Ask the Spirit of God to enlighten you, e.g.:
   'Lord, you enlighten every heart. Enlighten mine to recognise how you have been guiding me. Help me to distinguish those inspirations that came from You from those that came either from myself or from the Evil One.'
4. Were you aware of any promptings or inspirations during the day?
   – How did they affect you?
   – Were they associated with feelings of consolation or desolation?
   Pause now, and try to recall how you felt at the time.

– Recall these words of St Paul, 'The Spirit you received is not a spirit of fear' (2 Tm 1:7). Nor is it a spirit of morbid guilt, resentful anger, envy, jealousy, selfish pride, lust, etc.

– In retrospect, would it be true to say that such a negative impulse has led you to consent to some inappropriate thought, word, deed or omission?

– If so, acknowledge it to the Lord, and ask him with confidence for his forgiveness.

5. Recall the inspirations and promptings the Lord graced you with today.

– Thank him for them, and the Spirit-given ability to express them in deeds.

– If you failed to act upon them, however, tell the Lord you are sorry.

– Ask him to continue to guide you in the future.

14

TRANSFORMATION IN CHRIST

There has been a fundamental change in the way in which we look at reality. In former centuries there was a static non-historical world view. It emphasised universal principles and their implications for everyday living. For example, the different levels of hierarchical society – the monarchy, aristocracy and peasantry – were seen as an unchanging expression of the will of God. So, while the Christians of the time demonstrated the compassion and mercy of God by giving practical assistance to the poor they neither critiqued nor reformed the unjust structures of society which often made that poverty inevitable. In the modern era, hierarchical society has given way to one that is democratic, pluralist and secular. The traditional world view has been replaced by one which is evolutionary and dynamic in nature. It stresses such things as the rights of conscience, and the autonomy and freedom of the human person. Nowadays, besides giving practical assistance to the poor, Christians not only identify the unjust structures of society, they try to modify them. This change in world views was acknowledged by *The Church in the Modern World*, one of the documents of the Second Vatican Council. It stated that humankind has substituted 'a dynamic and more evolutionary concept of nature for a static one' (n.5). Another way of expressing this point is to say that instead of stressing the importance of *being*, as heretofore, nowadays we stress the importance of *becoming*.

Two approaches to spirituality
This paradigm shift has had a big impact on Christian spirituality. The centre of gravity has moved from the experience of religious authority to the authority of religious experience. Spirituality based on authority tends to be essentialist and programmatic in nature. It sees Christian perfection principally in terms of obedience, of the necessity of conforming in a docile way to a programme of

living recommended by the Church. It is inclined to stress the basic importance of texts such as, 'In the scroll of the book it is written of me, see God, I have come to do your will...If you keep my commandments, you will abide in my love, just as I have kept my Father's commandments and I abide in his love' (Hb 10:7; Jn 15:10). For example, speaking of Christian perfection, John Henry Newman said that it didn't require 'any extraordinary service, anything out of the way, or especially heroic.' The Cardinal went on to say, 'he is perfect who does the work of the day perfectly, and we need not go beyond this to seek for perfection.... If you ask me what you are to do in order to be perfect, I say, first – Do not lie in bed beyond the due time of rising; give your first thoughts to God; make a visit to the Blessed Sacrament; say the Angelus devoutly; eat and drink to God's glory; say the Rosary well; be recollected; keep out bad thoughts; make your evening meditation well; examine yourself daily; go to bed in good time, and you are already perfect.'[1]

Despite its undoubted merit, in our fast-changing world the programmatic model of spirituality is being replaced by a new, more existential one. It stresses the importance of such things as religious experience, personal and collective discernment, together with committed action for justice and liberation. Modern Christians are motivated not so much by a static notion of perfection, as by a heartfelt desire for spiritual transformation. They long to move away from negative influences of an environmental and an unconscious kind, in order to develop an intimate relationship with the deeper self, other people, creation, and God. There are a number of scripture texts which inspire existential models of spirituality such as 'your mind must be renewed in spirit so that you can put on the new man....you have stripped off your old behaviour with your old self, and you have put on the new self....in order to come...to the maturity, to the measure of the full stature of Christ' (Ep 2:23; Col 3:10; Ep 4:13). However, it is arguable that the following verse encapsulates the aim of modern spirituality: 'All of us with unveiled faces, seeing the glory of the Lord as though reflected in a mirror, are being transformed into the same image from one degree of glory to another; for this comes from the Lord; the Spirit' (2 Co 3:18). If

Newman was an exponent of programmatic Christianity, Thomas Merton was one of the most articulate exponents of the existentialist approach. He was aware that 'the self' had displaced the authority of objective truth as the focal point of contemporary spirituality where psychology and religion, nature and grace intersect. He wrote in *Seeds of Contemplation*: 'For me to be a saint means to be myself. Therefore the problem of sanctity and salvation is in fact the problem of finding out who I am and discovering my true self.' As we have already noted in chapter 9, Merton believed that people could only discover their true selves in and through relationship with God. 'The secret of my identity,' he wrote in characteristic fashion, 'is hidden in the love and mercy of God.'[2]

The three stages of spiritual transformation

So far in this book we have looked at the reality of diabolical evil, ways in which it can impinge on human life, and some of the practical means of overcoming it. In this chapter we will use the verse in 2 Corinthians 3:18, referred to above, to look at the threefold way in which we can overcome evil by being transformed into the image of Christ. Traditional Christian teaching has suggested that the spiritual life involves a threefold journey of inner transformation, i.e. that of the beginner, the proficient and the perfect. During the purgative stage people learn to identify and renounce sinful habits, addictions and worldly attachments. During the illuminative stage, they are enlightened. They have a connatural or intuitive understanding of the things of God and the Spirit. When the unitive stage is reached, people enjoy a loving union of their wills, if not their minds and imaginations, with the mystery of God as he is revealed in Christ.

In a sermon for Pentecost, St Aelred of Rievaulx (d.1167) related the three stages of growth to three stages in the life of Jesus. 'Contemplate in Christ three stages, as it were planned by his wonderful kindness, not for his benefit, but for ours. First, he was baptised, then he was transfigured, finally he was glorified. He was baptised in the Jordan, transfigured on the mountain, and glorified at length in heaven. At Christ's baptism the Holy Spirit was shown as a dove, at his transfiguration as a cloud, but after his resurrection as fire. Take these three stages to represent the three stages in the soul's progress: purification, illumination and rewarding. Christ's baptism represents our purification, his transfiguration our illumination, and his glorification our rewarding. We are purified by confession, we are illumined by contemplation, and we are rewarded by the fullness of charity.' In this chapter, I suggest that the three stages are implicit in 2 Corinthians 3:18. The unveiling of the face refers to the purgative stage. Seeing the glory of the Lord refers to the illuminative stage, while being transformed into the image of the Lord refers to the unitive stage. We will look at each of these in turn.

Unveiling the heart

What does Paul mean when he talks about 'unveiled faces'? If we go back two verses, we find that he had already given an explanation in 2 Corinthians 3:16. 'Whenever anyone turns to the Lord,' he comments, 'the veil is taken away.' The veil refers, therefore, to those things that harden the heart, thereby separating it from the Lord. As Jesus said, quoting the prophet Isaiah, 'this people's heart has become calloused; they hardly hear with their ears, and they have closed their eyes. Otherwise they might see with their eyes, hear with their ears, understand with their hearts and turn, and I would heal them' (Mt 13:15). There is also an echo of the Pauline verse in Matthew 6:22: 'The eye is the lamp of the body. If your eyes are good, your whole body will be full of light.'

The face is unveiled when pseudo-innocence is overcome through growing self-awareness. We have already looked at some of the ways in which this can occur in preceding chapters. Part 1 of *Intimacy and the Hungers of the Heart* deals with this subject, especially chapter 4, which is entitled 'The Pain of Self-Discovery'. By way of summary we can advert to a few relevant points. Firstly, the Lord can use our sufferings, life-crises, temptations and failings together with attention to such things as dreams, desires, feelings and affective attitudes to enable us to know ourselves better. Secondly, we unveil our hearts as we become aware of the inward fissure that divides the acceptable, lovable self from that which is rejected and despised. As we saw in an earlier chapter,

Freud and Jung have demonstrated how this can be a source of evil by preventing us loving either ourselves, or other people. This in turn, can lead us to project our own inner darkness on to other people. We see and reject in them the very things we fail to see or acknowledge in ourselves. Thirdly, we can unveil our hearts by carrying out Steps Four and Five of Alcoholics Anonymous, namely, by making 'a searching and fearless moral inventory of ourselves and admitting to God, to ourselves, and to another human being the exact nature of our wrongs.' I looked at what these steps might involve in chapters 8 and 9. Suffice it to say, that as far as Catholics are concerned, one powerful way of unveiling the heart is to receive the sacrament of reconciliation, in a conscientious way, at least a few times a year.

Beholding the Lord

In 2 Corinthians 3:18 Paul speaks about reflecting or seeing the glory of the Lord. I use both words deliberately, because the Greek word, *katoptrizomenoi*, can be translated either as 'to reflect', i.e. as in a mirror, or as 'to see, to behold, or to contemplate'. Both translations refer to important aspects of our relationship to Christ. As the heart is unveiled, it is better able to receive and to reflect the Glory of God, i.e. the red and white light of Christ's mercy and love which is hidden from those whose hearts are veiled by unacknowledged and unrepented sin. Scripture often talks about the divine glory. In John 1:14 we read: 'we have seen his glory, the glory as of a Father's only Son, full of grace and truth.' In Hebrews 1:3 we read: 'The Son is the radiance of God's glory and the exact representation of his being.' As the heart is unveiled, it becomes, in the words of Paul, the 'image and reflection of God' (1 Co 11:7).

This process of reflecting God's glory occurs as we contemplate his presence and power, especially as a result of reading and praying the scriptures in a meditative way. This is particularly true when it comes to the gospels. The words and actions of Christ are like so many panes in the stained-glass window of his humanity. When they are illumined by the light of the Spirit and perceived with the eyes of faith, they reveal what God is really like. As Jesus said in John 14:9, 'the one who sees me, sees the Father.' Because this is true, a verse of one hymn prays, 'In the scriptures, by the Spirit, may we see the Saviour's face, hear his word and heed his calling, know his will and grow in grace.' There are many ways in which this prayer can be answered, notably by using either the Benedictine or the Ignatian methods of contemplating God's word. If we wish to 'overcome evil' in the way Paul advises in Romans 12:21, we need to be armed with the 'sword of the Spirit, which is the word of God' (Ep 6:17). We do this by committing ourselves to a daily quiet time. Like Mary, we ponder God's word in our hearts. We can read a relevant passage in the Bible, look at the liturgical readings of the day or for the following Sunday, or use a suitable book such as *Daily Light*,[3] which contains thematic scripture readings for every day of the year.

As we encounter the Lord, especially in and through the scriptures, 'we are transformed', says St Paul in 2 Corinthians 3:18, 'into the same image.' In other words, when we contemplate Christ, our human form, afflicted as it is by sin and evil, is transformed. Through the action of God's Spirit, we acquire a new nature. Because Christ lives within our hearts we come to share in the holiness and goodness of his divinity. As the Seventh Sunday Preface puts it, 'so great was God's love, that he gave us his Son as our redeemer. He sent him as one like ourselves, though free from sin, that he might see and love in us what he sees and loves in Christ.' It is important to realise that instead of being a definitive event, it is a lifelong developmental process, one which needs to find practical expression in loving and virtuous deeds. It will only be complete when, as Paul reminds us in 1 Corinthians 13:12, 'we will see the Lord, not as in a mirror dimly, but face to face in glory.'

Another effect of the process of transformation is the fact that Christians are inwardly illumined. In the words of Ignatius of Loyola, people are enabled to have an 'intimate knowledge of Jesus Christ'. Speaking about himself, the founder of the Jesuits said, that as his relationship with the Lord matured, he was enlightened by the Spirit-given gift of understanding. In his *Autobiography* he describes how this occurred during his time at Manresa. Apparently one memorable day he went for a walk along the bank of the river Cardoner. At one point, 'he sat down for a little while and turned toward the water which was running deep. While he was seated there, the eyes of his understanding began to be opened; though he did not see any vision, he understood and knew many things, both spiritual things and matters of faith and learning, and this with so great an enlightenment that everything seemed new to him. Though there were many, he cannot set forth the details that he understood then, except that he experienced a great clarity in his understanding.'[4] To a greater or lesser extent, all those who are becoming proficient in the Christian life receive this kind of enlightenment, as St Paul wrote, 'What no eye has seen, nor ear heard, nor the human heart conceived...these things God has revealed to us through the Spirit; for the Spirit searches everything, even the depths of God' (1 Co 2:9-11).

In chapter 13 we saw how the gifts of wisdom and knowledge enable people to have a connatural or intuitive sense of the will of God. As a person grows closer to Christ through the inward action of the Holy Spirit, he or she develops an instinctive sense of what the purposes of God might be in the practical circumstances of everyday life. This kind of sixth-sense 'surpasses understanding' (Ep 3:19). No amount of human learning or reasoning can provide it. As Jesus said in Matthew 11:25, the Father has hidden his mind and will 'from the wise and intelligent and has revealed them to infants', i.e. those who, with complete trust, live in complete and utter dependence on him. Not only can this kind of illumination enable our everyday judgements and actions to be 'guided by the Spirit' (Ga 5:18), in its charismatic form it can enable us to know the apparently unknowable, e.g. who is going to be healed of what during a healing service.

For example, during a healing Mass in Northern Ireland, I saw a woman in my mind's eye. I could see what she looked like and what she was wearing. In my spirit I seemed to know where she was in the congregation and that she was suffering from a very painful back complaint. Without opening my eyes, I prayed for her over the public address. When the Mass concluded, two women came into the sacristy. One of them was the woman I had interceded for. It turned out that the other was her family doctor. She was able to verify that her patient had been suffering from a bad back, and that she had completely recovered after the prayer on her behalf. I have since discovered that the healing was permanent.

There is an interesting example of the charismatic gift of connatural knowledge in the Philokalia. St Anthony of the Desert told two monks that they should go down the road towards Egypt where they would find one dead man and another who was dying. The monks set out and found things just as Anthony had described. As Nicephorus the Solitary commented, 'You see that, through sobriety of the heart (i.e. through unveiling and contemplation), St Anthony was given divine vision and clairvoyance.'[5]

Growing from one degree of glory to another

As the process of transformation grows deeper, the person becomes more and more closely united to the One who cannot be grasped in either thought or image. As the Fourth Lateran Council said in the twelfth century, 'Between the Creator and creatures no similarity can be expressed without including a greater dissimilarity.' During the purgative and illuminative stages of transformation, Christians typically stress what can be known about God by means of thought and imagination. When they reach the unitive stage of transformation, many of them will continue to stress the importance of the mediating power of ideas and images. There is a graphic example of this kind of 'mediated immediacy', in chapter XVI of St Thérèse's *Autobiography of a Saint*. As she attests on the basis of personal experience, this sacramental approach can lead to mystical union with God.[6] However, there will always be others, who will be inclined to go beyond the limitations of concepts and symbols with their associated feelings, in order to stress the incomprehensibility of God. They are inspired to pray in words like these, 'Serene Light, shining in the ground of my being. Draw me to Yourself! Draw me past the snare of the senses, out of the mazes of the mind. Free me from symbols, from words, that I may discover the Signified, the Word Unspoken, in the darkness which veils the ground of my being.'[7]

St Gregory of Nyssa (c.330-c.395), a brother of St Basil, was one of the most profound and influential spiritual writers in the early Church. He indicated how Moses experienced an answer to such a prayer. 'To the great Moses, God first appeared in light (i.e. the illuminative stage of growth). Afterwards God spoke to him through a cloud. Finally, when he had ascended to greater and more perfect heights, Moses saw God in darkness. All this signifies that our passage from false and errant notions of God is a passage from darkness to light. A closer consideration of hidden things through things which can be seen, leads the soul to that nature which cannot be seen: and this is like a cloud overshadowing all that has outward appearances, in order to lead the soul on and accustom it to the dark (the unitive stage of growth). The soul that thus climbs into the heights, leaving behind everything that human nature can attain by itself, enters into the sanctuary of the knowledge of God, surrounded on every side by the divine darkness. And there everything that can be seen or understood having been left outside, nothing is left for the soul to see but that which is invisible and incomprehensible. And therein God is hidden, for scripture says of the lawgiver: Moses entered "the darkness where God is" (Ex 24:18).'[8]

Many years ago, as I emerged from a drowsy state of mind, I had an imageless, conceptless awareness, not only of the contingency of my own existence, but of that of all things. I was in awe of the fact that something rather than nothing exists, and that I was part of that something. It seemed to me, that all existence was intrinsically good. Implicit in this experience was a twofold intuition. Firstly, neither I, nor anything else, was the adequate explanation of its own existence. Secondly, God was the One who created all things and upheld them in the goodness of being from one moment to the next. More recently, I had a similar experience. Again it occurred in that twilight zone between sleeping and waking. On this occasion, however, I was primarily aware of the presence of God. I seemed to have an immediate awareness of my being connected, without the mediation of image or concept, to the incomprehensible mystery of the Mysterious Other. Not surprisingly, this experience was associated with an inner sense of peace and reassurance. Since then, I have been attracted to those spiritual writers who suggest practical ways of deepening one's sense of union with the Lord without the mediating role of ideas and symbols.

For example, in the *Cloud of Unknowing*, the anonymous medieval author suggests a way of making this possible. Like Cassian, who was quoted in the chapter on overcoming temptation, he advocates the use of a mantra. He writes; 'If you want to gather all your desire into one simple word that the mind can easily retain, choose a short word rather than a long one. A one syllable word such as 'God' or 'love' is best. But choose one that is meaningful to you. Then fix it in your mind so that it will remain there come what may. This word will be your defence in conflict and peace. Use it to beat off the cloud of darkness above you and to subdue all distractions, consigning them to the cloud of forgetting beneath you. Should some thought go on annoying you, demanding to know what you are doing, answer with this one word alone. If your mind begins to intellectualise over the meaning and connotations of this little word, remind yourself that its value lies in its simplicity. Do this and I assure you that these thoughts will vanish. Why? Because you have refused to develop them with arguing.'[9]

As devout Christians contemplate the Lord in these and other ways, they are transformed into the divine image and are progressively delivered from egocentric pride and all its attendant evils. Describing people in the unitive stage, Evelyn Underhill has written in *Mystics of the Church*: 'Whereas in the earlier stages they saw and moved towards the life of Spirit, now they find themselves immersed in it, inspired and directed in all their actions by the indwelling love of God. This...brings with it astonishing reserves of energy and endurance, a power of dealing with persons and events far beyond the self's 'natural' capacities.'[10] Indeed, some of them have become literally radiant with the light of the Spirit. In his interesting book, *Cosmic Consciousness*, Canadian doctor Richard Bucke described how many people, such as St John of the Cross, who had reached the unitive stage of transformation, were occasionally transfigured by visible rays of light. A biographer reports that one night during

John's imprisonment by members of his own order, 'His cell became filled with light seen by the bodily eye.... The friar who kept him went as usual to see that the prisoner was safe, and witnessed the heavenly light with which the cell was flooded.'[11] On a number of occasions in my own life I have had the privilege of meeting Christians like Mother Teresa of Calcutta and Jean Vanier, who were metaphorically, if not literally, aglow with the light of love. They are credible witnesses, in today's troubled world, to him who said, 'I am the light of the world. Whoever follows me will never walk in darkness but will have the light of life' (Jn 8:12). It is this light, and this light alone which can increasingly and triumphantly overcome the darkness of sin and evil which afflicts humanity.

NOTES

Introduction

1. London, Pan Books, 1967, pp. 325-327.
2. 'Deliver us from Evil', General Audience, 15 November 1972, L'*Osservatore Romano,* 23 November 1972.

Chapter 1: A Time of Adversity

1. Quoted in *Open Your Hearts to Mary Queen of Peace* (Milan, The Association of the friends of Medjugorje, 1986), p.14. Apparently Pope Leo XII had a similar message a century ago when, in a vision, he saw the Church being attacked by demons. As a result he introduced the prayer to St Michael the Archangel.
2. Pope Paul VI said in a talk entitled 'Making Religion Flourish in our Time', 'Statistics speak clearly: religion is losing ground', *Pope Paul and the Spirit,* ed. O'Connor, (Notre Dame, Ave Maria Press, 1978), p. 186.
3. London, Penguin Books, 1964.
4. Johannes Jorgensen, *St Francis of Assisi* (New York, Image Books, 1955), p. 42.

Chapter 2: Understanding the Experience of Evil

1. London, Arkana, 1990, pp. 190-191.
2. Fogarty, Ryan, Lee, Eds. *Irish Values and Attitudes: The Irish Report of the European Value Systems Study* (Dublin, Dominican Publications, 1984), p. 125.
3. 'Deliver Us from Evil', General Audience of Pope Paul VI, 15 November 1972, as reprinted in L'*Osservatore Romano* (23 November 1972).
4. 'The Second Coming', from *Selected Poetry,* ed. A.N. Jeffares, (London, Papermac, 1962), pp. 99-100.

Chapter 3: Modern Science and the Devil

1. Bernard Ruffin, *Padre Pio: The True Story* (Indiana, Sunday Visitor, 1982), p. 93.
2. *Leonardo da Vinci and a Memory of his Childhood*, in SE 11, p. 123.
3. 'Psychotherapists or the Clergy?' in *Psychology and Western Religion* (London, Ark, 1988), p.202.
4. New York, Simon and Schuster, 1983, p. 195.
5. Quoted by Lincoln Barnett in *The Universe and Dr Einstein* (New York, Bantam Books, 1980), p.108.
6. Oxford, Oxford University Press, 1983, p. 44.
7. *The Holographic Universe* (New York, Harper Perennial, 1992), pp 205-8.
8. *The Psychopathic God: Adolf Hitler* (New York, Mentor, 1977).
9. 'Adolf Hitler's Childhood: From Hidden to Manifest Horror', in *For Your Own Good* (New York, Farrar, Straus, Giroux, 1980), pp. 142-195.

Chapter 4: To the Devil with Psychology

1. *Leonardo Da Vinci and a Memory of his Childhood*, op. cit., p. 123.
2. *The Psychopathic God: Adolf Hitler*, op.cit., p. 439.
3. *The Ghost in the Machine* (London, Pan Books, 1967), p. 269.
4. *Civilisation in Transition* (New York, Pantheon Books, 1964), p. 212.
5. At p. 207.
6. 'Psychology and Religion', in *Collected Works,* Vol. 11, p. 335.

Chapter 5: Does the Devil Exist?

1. *Encounter With God* (London, Hodder and Stoughton, 1972), p. 242.
2. *The New Jerome Biblical Commentary* (New Jersey, Prentice Hall, 1990), p. 1321.
3. New York, Paulist Press, 1990, pp. 70-71.
4. London, Geoffrey Chapman, 1994, pp. 41-42.
5. London, SCM Press, 1975, p. 44.

6. *Christian Faith and Demonology*, in *Vatican Council II: More Postconciliar Documents* (Dublin, Dominican Publications, 1982)
7. New York, Doubleday, 1974
8. *Eternal Life* (London, Fount, 1985), p. 167. Haag has written, 'The Evil One is only a myth for human sin.'
9. *Eternal Life*, op.cit., p. 167.
10. 'Angels', in *Encyclopaedia of Theology: A Concise Sacramentum Mundi*, ed. K. Rahner (London, Burns and Oates, 1975), p.9.
11. *Christian Mysticism: The Future of a Tradition* (New York, Pueblo, 1984), pp. 347-359.
12. *Spiritual Theology* (London, Sheed and Ward, 1982), pp. 404-415.
13. Quoted in Paul Qual's 'Angels and Demons: The Teaching of IV Lateran', *Theological Studies* XLII, No. 1, March 1981.
14. Op., cit., p. 45.
15. *Vatican Council II: More Postconciliar Documents* (Dublin, Dominican Publications, 1982), pp.456-485.
16. *Studia Liturgica* 10 (1974).

Chapter 6: Possession and Exorcism Explained

1. The Church's thinking on this subject was contained in a letter from the Congregation for Faith and Doctrine which was addressed to Catholic bishops on 29 September 1985. It prohibits lay people from performing solemn exorcisms, and says that in accordance with Canon 1172 of the Code of Canon Law, bishops should appoint a priest who is good, holy, learned, and prudent for this purpose.
2. Quoted by Kelly in *The Devil, Demonology and Witchcraft* (New York, Doubleday, 1974), p. 92.
3. Kelly, op. cit., p. 98.
4. *St Francis de Sales: A Testimony by St Chantal*, ed. Elisabeth Stopp (London, Faber & Faber, 1967), p. 150.

Chapter 7: Tactics of the Evil One

1. For more on this point see, K. Rahner, 'The Two Standards,' in *Meditations on Priestly Life* (London, Sheed and Ward, Stagbooks, 1974), pp. 170-179.

2. *The Way of the Heart: Desert Spirituality and Contemporary Ministry* (London, Darton, Longman & Todd, 1981), pp. 22-23.

3. *Addiction and Grace* (New York, Harper and Row, 1988), p. 14.

4. London, Picador, 1993, ch. 1, pp. 1-16.

5. 'Encyclical Letter of Pope John Paul II, *Veritatis Splendor* (The Splendour of Truth)', *The Daily Telegraph*, 6 October 1993. It is interesting to note that in 1990 Chief Rabbi Jonathan Sacks said (in his BBC Reith lecture, no. 2), entitled, 'The Demoralisation of Discourse', that 'The orthodoxies of our time are that morality is a private affair, a matter of personal choice, and that the state must be morally neutral' (*The Listener*, 22 November 1990).

6. 'Progress and Decline', in *Method in Theology* (London, Darton, Longman & Todd, 1972), pp. 52-55, and *Insight: A Study of Human Understanding* (New York, Longman, 1958), pp. 687-730.

Chapter 8: The Awareness of Sin

1. Edward O'Connor, *Pope Paul and The Spirit* (Notre Dame, Ave Maria Press, 1978), p 177.

2. O'Connor, idem., p.69.

3. Book XIV, sec. 6

4. For more on this, see John Glasser, 'Conscience and Superego: A Key Distinction,' *Theological Studies*, no. 32, 1971.

5. Joyce Riddick, *Treasures in Earthen Vessels: The Vows* (Slough, St Paul Publications, 1984), p. 50.

Chapter 9: Victory over Sin

1. Quoted by Grace Jantzen in *Julian of Norwich* (London, SPCK, 1987), p. 209.

2. Quoted by J. Higgins in *Thomas Merton on Prayer* (New York, Image, 1971), p. 59.

3. *Glimpse into Glory* (New York, Logos, 1979)

4. Kuhlmann, idem.
5. Croydon, Movement Books, 1972, p. 39.
6. Conference on 'Charity', 30 May 1659, *Conferences of St Vincent de Paul* (Philadelphia, Vincentian, 1963), p. 387.
7. 'Life after Life', in *Thinking Allowed: Conversations on the Leading Edge of Knowledge*, ed. Jeffrey Mishlove (Berkley, Council Oak Books, 1992), pp. 356-363.

Chapter 10: Freedom from Addiction

1. San Francisco, Harper and Row, 1988, pp. 24-25.
2. *Addiction and Grace,* op.cit., pp. 36-37.
3. 'Psychotherapists or Clergy', in *Psychology and Western Religion,* op.cit., p.208-209.
4. Quoted by D. Linn, S.F. Linn and M. Linn in *Belonging: Bonds of Healing and Recovery* (New York, Paulist Press, 1993), pp. 9-10.
5. *Addiction and Grace* , op.cit., p.3.
6. San Francisco, Harper and Row, 1982, p. 132
7. *Care of Mind, Care of Spirit: Psychiatric Dimensions of Spiritual Direction* (New York, Harper & Row, 1982), p.132.
8. San Francisco, Harper and Row, 1982, p. 6.
9. *Belonging: Bonds of Healing and Recovery,* op.cit., p.64.
10. *Pass it On* (New York, Alcoholics Anonymous World Services, 1984), p.384.
11. Idem, pp.10-11.
12. Dublin, Columba Press, 1991, pp. 209-229.

Chapter 11: Inner Healing

1. Quoted by Alan Bullock in *Hitler and Stalin: Parallel Lives* London, Fontana Books, 1993), p.4.
2. *Banished Knowledge* (New York, Doubleday, 1990), pp.13 & 170.
3. *Clinical Theology: A Theological and Psychological Basis to Clinical Pastoral Care* (London, Darton Longman & Todd, 1986), p. 12.
4. Ann Arbor, Word of Life, 1977, p. 73.

5.   *Healing the Shame that Binds You* (Deerfield Beach, Health Communications, 1988), p. 97.
6.   New York, Paulist Press, 1974, pp. 51-52.

Chapter 12: Resisting Temptation

1.   *Collected Letters and Conferences,* ed. Coste (X.8)
2.   *Summa Theologiae: A Concise Translation,* ed. McDermott, (London, Methuen, 1991), p. 158.
3.   Dublin, Veritas Publications, 1994, 2846-2849.
4.   *De Oratione* 29: p. 11, 544 C-D quoted in the Catechism, op.cit., p. 606.
5.   Jules A. Toner's translation of 'Rules for the Discernment of Spirits, from the Spiritual Exercises', nn. 325-327, in *Women's Spirituality: Resources for Christian Development,* ed. J. W. Conn (New York, Paulist Press, 1986), pp. 212-213.
6.   n. 325
7.   n. 326
8.   'On Resisting Temptation,' bk. 1, chapter 13, par 5.
9.   *Common Rules of The Congregation of the Mission,* chapter 2, par. 16.
10. 'Conference X on Prayer' in *The Fire and the Cloud: An Anthology of Catholic Spirituality,* ed. D. A. Fleming (London, Geoffrey Chapman, 1978), pp.28-41.
11. Op.cit., p.35.
12. Op.cit., p.38.
13. Quoted in F. C. Happold's *Prayer and Meditation: Their Nature and Practice* (London, Penguin Books, 1971), p. 133.

Chapter 13: Discernment of Spirits

1.   *The Holy Spirit: Growth of a Biblical Tradition* (New York, Paulist Press, 1976), p. 200.
2.   See Pat Collins, 'Devotion to the Holy Spirit', in *The Joy of Belonging* (Galway, Campus, 1993), pp. 93-94.
3.   *Conferences of Saint Vincent de Paul,* op.cit., p. 213.
4.   Dublin, Columba Press, 1991, pp. 96-111.
5.   *Spiritual Exercises* (32).

6. 'Living by the Spirit,' 23 June 1971, in *Pope Paul and the Spirit*, ed. Edward O'Connor (Notre Dame, Ave Maria Press, 1978), p.167.
7. *The Holy Spirit*, op.cit., p. 154.
8. *Summa Theologiae: A Concise Translation*, op.cit., p. 370.
9. *Christian Perfection and Contemplation* (St Louis, Herder Book Co., 1946), p. 271.
10. *Conferences of Saint Vincent de Paul*, op.cit., p. 472.
11. *Directoria Exercitiorum Spiritualium*, in MHSJ [12], on p.72.
12. *The Autobiography of St Ignatius Loyola with Related Documents* (New York, Harper & Row, 1974), p. 24.
13. *Spiritual Exercises* (318).

Chapter 14: Transformation in Christ

1. An extract from *Meditations and Devotions* quoted in *The Essential Newman*, Ed. V. Blehl (New York, New American Library, 1963), pp. 337-338.
2. Wheathampstead, Anthony Clarke, 1972, p. 25.
3. New International Version (London, Hodder and Stoughton, 1984)
4. *The Autobiography of St Ignatius Loyola with Related Documents* (New York, Harper & Row, 1974), p.39
5. *Writings from the Philokalia: On Prayer of the Heart* (London, Faber & Faber, 1992), p. 24.
6. See *Intimacy and the Hungers of the Heart*, op.cit., chapter 12.
7. Phyllis Campbell's prayer in F. C. Happold's *Prayer and Meditation: Their Nature and Practice* (London, Penguin, 1971), p. 122
8. See *Commentary on the Song of Songs* 11 (PG 44. 1000C).
9. Introductory commentary and translation of Ira Progoff (New York, Dell Publishing, 1957), chapter 37, par. 2., pp. 147-148.
10. Cambridge, James Clarke, 1975, p. 27.
11. New York, Dutton, 1969, p. 143.

SUGGESTED READING

'The Christian Faith and Demonology' in *Vatican Council II: More Postconciliar Documents,* ed. Austin Flannery OP (Dublin, Dominican Publications, 1982), pp. 456-485.

'The Fall of the Angels', in *Catechism of the Catholic Church* (Dublin, Veritas, 1994), pp. 88-89; 607-608.

Léon-Joseph Cardinal Suenens, *Renewal and the Powers of Darkness* (London, DLT, 1983)

Raymond Brown, *Responses to 101 Questions on the Bible* (New York, Paulist Press, 1990), questions 49-51.

Raymond Brown, *An Introduction to New Testament Christology* (London, Geoffrey Chapman, 1994), pp. 41-42.

Matthew and Dennis Linn, Eds., *Deliverance Prayer* (New York, Paulist Press, 1981)

Pat Collins CM, 'Faith and Deliverance from Evil', sec. 3., *Finding Faith in Troubled Times* (Dublin, Columba Press, 1993), pp. 102-147.

Michael Scanlan and Randall Cirner, *Deliverance From Evil Spirits* (Ann Arbor, Michigan, Servant Books, 1980)

Pat Collins CM, 'Exorcism and the Falling Phenomenon', ch. 10, *Maturing in the Spirit* (Dublin, Columba Press, 1991), pp. 141-149.

Tom Smail, 'Into His Likeness' in *Reflected Glory: The Spirit in Christ and Christians* (London, Hodder & Stoughton, 1975), pp. 24-35.

Sean Fagan, *Has Sin Changed?* (Dublin, Gill & Macmillan, 1978)

Jordan Aumann, 'Conversion from Sin', in *Spiritual Theology* (London, Sheed & Ward, 1982), pp. 139-176

Benedict Groeschel, 'The First Stage of the Spiritual Life', in *Spiritual Passages: The Psychology of Spiritual Development* (New York, Paulist Press, 1982), pp. 103-135.

Linn, Linn & Linn, *Belonging: Bonds of Healing and Recovery* (New Jersey, Paulist Press, 1993)

Leanne Payne, *Restoring the Christian Soul Through Healing Prayer* (Eastbourne, Kingsway, 1992)

Gerald May, *Addiction and Grace* (New York, Harper & Row, 1988)

Michael Scanlon, *The Power in Penance: Confession and the Holy Spirit* (Notre Dame, Indiana, Ave Maria Press, 1978)

Evelyn Underhill, *Mystics of the Church* (Cambridge, James Clarke & Co., 1975), ch. 1.

INDEX